T0328798

Cambridge Elements

Elements in the Gothic
edited by
Dale Townshend
Manchester Metropolitan University
Angela Wright
University of Sheffield

MARY ROBINSON
AND THE GOTHIC

Jerrold E. Hogle
University of Arizona

CAMBRIDGE
UNIVERSITY PRESS

Shaftesbury Road, Cambridge CB2 8EA, United Kingdom

One Liberty Plaza, 20th Floor, New York, NY 10006, USA

477 Williamstown Road, Port Melbourne, VIC 3207, Australia

314–321, 3rd Floor, Plot 3, Splendor Forum, Jasola District Centre, New Delhi – 110025, India

103 Penang Road, #05–06/07, Visioncrest Commercial, Singapore 238467

Cambridge University Press is part of Cambridge University Press & Assessment, a department of the University of Cambridge.

We share the University's mission to contribute to society through the pursuit of education, learning and research at the highest international levels of excellence.

www.cambridge.org
Information on this title: www.cambridge.org/9781009160872

DOI: 10.1017/9781009160889

First published 2023

A catalogue record for this publication is available from the British Library.

ISBN 978-1-009-16087-2 Paperback
ISSN 2634-8721 (online)
ISSN 2634-8713 (print)

Cambridge University Press & Assessment has no responsibility for the persistence or accuracy of URLs for external or third-party internet websites referred to in this publication and does not guarantee that any content on such websites is, or will remain, accurate or appropriate.

Mary Robinson and the Gothic

Elements in the Gothic

DOI: 10.1017/9781009160889
First published online: March 2023

Jerrold E. Hogle
University of Arizona
Author for correspondence: Jerrold E. Hogle, hogle@arizona.edu

Abstract: Celebrated as an actress on the London stage (1776–80) and notorious as the mistress of the Prince of Wales (1779–80), Mary Darby Robinson had to write to support herself from the mid-1780s until her death in 1800. She mastered a wide range of styles, published prolifically, and became the poetry editor of the *Morning Post*. As her writing developed across the 1790s, she increasingly used the motifs of Gothic fiction and drama descended from Horace Walpole's *Castle of Otranto* (1764). These came to pervade her late novels and poems so much that she even wrote her autobiography as a Gothic romance. She also deployed them to critique the ideologies of male dominance and the forms of writing in which they appeared. This progression culminated in her final collection of verses, *Lyrical Tales* (1800), where she Gothically exposes the conflicted underpinnings in the now-famous *Lyrical Ballads* (1798) by Wordsworth and Coleridge.

Keywords: Mary Darby Robinson, the Gothic, the Rights of Women, French Revolutionary writings, the "English Sappho"

ISBNs: 9781009160872 (PB), 9781009160889 (OC)
ISSNs: 2634-8721 (online), 2634-8713 (print)

For
Aedan
and the entire Hogle-Brown-Boeckman clan

Contents

A Note on Texts

All citations from her writings here come from *The Works of Mary Robinson* in eight volumes (abbreviated *WMR*), edited, with introductions and notes (to which I am often indebted), by William D. Brewer (general editor), Daniel Robinson, Dawn M. Vernoy-Epp, Sharon M. Setzer, Orianne Smith, Julie A. Shaffer, and Hester Davenport (London: Pickering and Chatto, 2009–10). All her texts – and some introductions and notes in these volumes – are cited by *WMR* volume and page number, and her poems are cited by line numbers as well, with her Gothic play (and all plays) cited by act, scene, and line numbers. All other citations refer to entries in the Bibliography at the end of this Element. The works there are cited in my text by last name and page number, with a year of publication being added only in those cases where I refer to multiple texts by the same author. For a reliable full chronology of Robinson's life, see *WMR* 1: xxxiii–xxxviii.

1 A Gothic Life

When Mary Darby Robinson (Figure 1) died on December 26, 1800 – having been a prolific poet, novelist, essayist, playwright, editor, critic, activist, leading major-theater actress (1776–80), and mistress to the Prince of Wales (1779–80) and other prominent men – she left unfinished an autobiography soon filled out and edited by her daughter Maria, likely aided by the poet Samuel Jackson Pratt (*WMR* 7: xix–xxv). It was published in 1801 as *Memoirs of the Late Mrs. Mary Robinson, Written by Herself* (7: 193–294). As several scholars have noted, most of it, even the "Continuation" half, reads like a Gothic novel, "with its plot of the tortured, long-suffering heroine ... in a world of terrifying torments" (Mellor 250; see also Close 172–175, 180–185). It begins by situating her birth in 1756 (possibly 1757; see *WMR* 1: xvi), not just in the "Minster-house" in Bristol where it happened, but within the towering "gothic structure" that encompasses it (*WMR* 7: 193). Even the house "was built" only "partly of modern architecture," since its "back was supported by the ancient cloisters of St. Augustine's," and that meant that the "gloomy" birth-room had "been a part of the original monastery" while the rest of the house now seems to sprout outward into modernity (193). The adjoining "cloisters" were parts of a "ruin" left by violent past upheavals, including the expulsion of the "monks" after the Reformation and (Robinson believed) a "cannonading" in 1653 (see *WMR* 7: 359–360 n.3). It is precisely because of this contradictory setting, explicitly called "dark, Gothic" and turned into a backdrop by a former stage performer, that the writer's "contemplative mind" is filled "at this moment ... with melancholy awe" (193). On one level, this opening strives to counter the coverage of Robinson as sexually profligate by claiming that her origins established a mindset of "mournful meditation" as the truest ground of her being (193). Such a claim extends a widespread ideology of the "architectural imagination" that, especially since the 1740s, increasingly came to pervade English aesthetics and saw Gothic structures, remaining or revived, as calling "up in the perceiver" certain "trains of thought" (Townshend 14) that quite often included Robinson's "melancholy awe."

On another level, this opening in the *Memoirs* also recalls the antique settings in the Gothic romances of Clara Reeve, Sophia Lee, Charlotte Smith, Ann Radcliffe, and others from the late 1770s–90s (see Mellor) and their roots in Horace Walpole's *The Castle of Otranto* (1764), the first fiction to call itself "A Gothic Story" in its second edition (1765; Walpole 2003: 63). That is especially so when the *Memoirs* emphasize how Robinson's birth-chamber was "supported" by the "arches" of a once-Catholic monastery, even though that room was part of a "modern" private house (*WMR* 7: 193). This description pulls her birth emphatically in two directions, making it and her look backward and forward like the two faces of the ancient Roman god Janus. In doing so, it repeats what Radcliffe emphasizes about many of

Figure 1 *Portrait of Mrs. Mary Robinson, née Darby* by Sir Joshua
Reynolds (1782).

the Gothic settings of her novels. In *A Sicilian Romance* (1790), the "mass of Gothic
architecture" that is another "abbey of St. Augustine," this one on the island of
Radcliffe's title, rises up "in proud sublimity" out of "the surrounding shades" as if
the spectator were looking back toward the past; to the modern "beholder,"
however, it appears as a hollowed-out, though magnificent, shell – what the
Bristol "ruins" are for Robinson – emptied of the "gross indulgences" and the
"clouds of prejudice" played out by "the priest, the nobleman, and the sovereign" of
"past ages," now rightly dissipated by the forward-looking "sun of science"
(Radcliffe 1993: 116), especially for enlightened Protestants of the later 1700s
(including Mary Darby, baptized an Anglican in 1758; *WMR* 1: xvi).

By invoking Radcliffe's Gothicized "sublimity," moreover, Robinson's
Memoirs continue, like her Gothic predecessors, the particular sense of that
term in Edmund Burke's *Philosophical Enquiry* on *the Sublime and Beautiful*
(1757). There vast gloomy scenes and dark ruins, especially in verbal art linking
them to bygone eras, arouse in spectators the fear of death, suggested by the

death of the past behind what remains. This is the "terror" that animates the aesthetic response that is Burke's sublime, in which "the mind is . . . entirely filled with its object" and pulled toward the death that the object suggests (Clery and Miles 113). But, especially given the distance of words from their referents, Burke's sublimity can still be "delightful," albeit tinged with some "melancholy" sense of loss, because art, more modern than its death-laden objects, can distance represented entities from any past "destruction" (Clery and Miles 121). All of this is echoed when Robinson writes of being born right at the juncture where ruins from now-absent history appear to sprout modern architecture while leaving a suspect antiquity in view. This very crux is what Walpole uses to define his new mode in his second *Otranto* Preface of 1765. The "Gothic Story" is for him a "blend" of "the two kinds of romance, the ancient and modern," in which the supernatural, chivalric, pastoral, and Catholic "ancient" strain, though still visible and enticing, is distanced as attractive and imaginative but ultimately "unnatural" for 1760s readers; "modern" fiction, by contrast, increasingly urban and mercantile, draws us toward the "rules of probability" accepted in the eighteenth century as part of "common life" rooted in more natural Protestant knowledge based on empirical perception (Walpole 2003: 65; see also Hogle 2019). No wonder Robinson highlights "the horrors of Walpole" right up front in one of her earliest novels (*WMR* 2: 347). Her *Memoirs*, like her Gothic writings in general, do not just echo the Gothic broadly defined. They pointedly extend the Janus-faced foundations of the Walpolean Gothic and its late-eighteenth-century progeny.

It is hardly surprising, then, that these *Memoirs* wax most Gothic and Walpolean when Robinson writes about major transitions and motivators in her life. When, from 1765–7, her father, Nicholas Darby, plunged his family from prosperity into debtor's prison by attempting a "fishery on the coast of Labrador" while continuing lavish spending, it is as if "potent witchery possessed his brain" with "its magic," since he was inclined toward "romantic" fantasies; yet, since he grew up "accustomed to a sea life," he "formed plans for the increase of wealth" based on his experience with seagoing, all the while hiding the "dreadful secret" of a "Mistress" (*WMR* 7: 197–198). Thus torn, like his daughter writing about her father, between "ancient" beliefs and "modern" internal drives, Nicholas resembles Walpole's Manfred, Prince of Otranto, who feels impelled by "his reliance on ancient prophecies" but also the "ambition" growing inside him (Walpole 2003: 149) to force a marriage between himself and Isabella, the betrothed of his now-dead son and the daughter of the Marquis Frederic, a rival claimant for the throne of Otranto (79–81, 120). This deceptive gambit, like Darby's, is flagrantly adulterous (since Manfred is still married) and obscures deep secrets: in *Otranto*'s case the murder of Alfonso, the Castle's founder, by Manfred's grandfather covered up by a "fictitious will," the exposure of which shows Manfred to be a false heir and uncovers an "authentic writing" revealing the existence of that founder's wife from whom the true heir has descended (164). Such conflicted villainy in Nicholas, so like Manfred's in its basic structure, is further seen by the *Memoirs* as exacerbated by Robinson's mother. She is written to be like Manfred's wife, Hippolita, who pitifully tries to dissuade her husband from extremes that could hurt the family but is ineffectually "obedient" to his "authority" in the end (147). Hester Darby is thus portrayed as "devoted" like Hippolita to the point of "too unlimited indulgence" with both husband and children (*WMR* 7: 197). One consequence is that young Mary and her brothers have been "little served to arm their breast against the perpetual arrows of mortal vicissitude" to come (7:197). This Hippolitan failing turns out to be one principal reason, Robinson now believes, why her mind's "original bent" became, quite early, too interwoven with "the progressive evils of a too acute sensibility" (7: 196).

The Gothic and Sensibility

By moving into this register, too – which Robinson had already done in her poetry (see McGann 94–116) – her *Memoirs* show how the Gothic came to her in the 1790s as already inflected with the philosophy of sensibility, infused somewhat into the characters of *Otranto* but inseparable from the Walpolean Gothic by the time of Radcliffe's romances (1789–97). Descending from the Earl of Shaftesbury's assertion of human altruism against the dominance of self-interest argued by Thomas Hobbes and from John Locke's empiricism, where all knowledge comes through sense-impressions and the feelings they arouse (hence "modern" in Walpole's scheme), this ideology was "generalized from the theories" of "David Hume and Adam Smith" (Poovey 307) and proliferated extensively in poems, plays, and novels well known to Robinson. It especially supported the ideals of the supposedly self-made middle class by associating self-realization with the individual "sensibility's capacity both to move and be moved" and the willingness of people "to face one another, adopt another's points of view," and thereby "modify passion into sentiment" (Chandler xvii). As Mary Poovey has shown, this ideology offered women "undeniable power" and new value during Robinson's lifetime, highlighting their supposedly greater capacity to feel; but it also made women (including women writers) draw back from excess feeling, including unrestrained sexuality, so that they could be seen as preserving the "sentimental values and behavior traditionally associated with paternalistic society" (Poovey 309). Women were thus positioned, like Robinson at birth, in another tug-of-war between the ancient and the modern that made depictions of women and their sensibilities immediately compatible with Janus-faced Gothic fiction. Hence Isabella in *Otranto*, as she flees from Manfred's predations, is torn between "her heart prompt[ing] her" to "go and prepare Hippolita for [a] cruel destiny" and escaping into the dark "subterraneous passage which led from the vaults of the castle to the church" (the option she chooses); there, in a scene that set a standard for the Gothic imperiling of women, "every murmur struck her with a new terror" because, while her feelings do reach maximum intensity, she is caught in the dark between two old patriarchal institutions, fearing confinement in both (Walpole 2003: 82). By the height of Radcliffe's writing career, this conflict became intensified by the warning that too much "delicacy of sentiment" could trap women into being "objects of contempt" that reinforce male control, to quote Mary Wollstonecraft's *A Vindication of the Rights of Woman* (1792; Wollstonecraft 1967: 34). Consequently, Radcliffe's *The Mysteries of Udolpho* (1794) directly anticipates the "too acute sensibility" of Robinson's *Memoirs* when Emily St. Aubert finds in herself "uncommon delicacy of mind, warm affections, and ready benevolence, but" also, echoing her father's warnings, "a degree of susceptibility too exquisite to admit of lasting peace" (Radcliffe 1998*b*: 5).

This combination of cultural schemes that both pull in contrary directions – the contest between ancient and modern in the Gothic and the valuing up and valuing down of women's feelings in the aesthetic of sensibility – therefore reappear in how Robinson's *Memoirs* describe the most (in)famous turns in her life following the 1760s. Soon after David Garrick first observes her talent for acting, probably in 1772 (*WMR* 1: xxxv), "he appeared to me as one who possessed more power, both to awe and attract," like an ancient authority-figure, "than any man I ever met" (7: 206). Similarly, as she remembers it, when she played "Perdita" (the "lost one"), which became her best-known role, in a command performance of Garrick's condensation of Shakespeare's *The Winter's Tale* on December 3, 1779 (1: xxxv), "my eyes met those of the Prince of Wales" right "as the curtain was falling," and he gave her "a look, that *I never shall forget*" from an elevated box conveying ancient royal power that looked down on paid commercial performers in a modern adaptation (7: 254). Both these scenes as written look back to the "physiognomy" of the monk Schedoni, the title character in Radcliffe's *The Italian* (1797): his "eyes were so piercing that they seemed to penetrate . . . into the hearts of men" and especially women, with hints of both "something terrible" in his past and yet an awesome seduc-tiveness that could "triumph" over onlookers with "astonishing facility" (Radcliffe 1998*a*: 34–35). As a result, these life-changing male gazes in the *Memoirs* arouse Robinson's sensibility toward both a "gratifying" flattery that promises "enchanting hours" (*WMR* 7: 204–207) and an awe tinged with fear that she could be seduced into losing what little self-determination she has. Prone to a "restless peevishness of tone," Garrick commands that Robinson "frequent the theater as much as possible," whether she wants to or not, before she debuts (7: 206), and the Prince requires that, at his first nighttime walks with her, she costume herself in "the male attire" from the "breeches" roles she has often enacted (7: 257). This last hint of performative female freedom mixed with enforced patriarchal orders soon becomes a step that the "Continuation" of the *Memoirs* sees – since Robinson's own manuscript stops after this point – as one of several that ultimately "rendered her but too obnoxious to a thousand errors and perils" (7: 259), very like those that beset Walpole-to-Radcliffe heroines from Isabella on.

Appearance versus "Reality"

These conflicts within the Gothic and sensibility are bound up in the *Memoirs*, moreover, with the equally "obnoxious" distance between appearance and reality. Even the latter for Robinson is rarely grounded in certainty because of conflicting impressions and words – for Ferdinand de Saussure "signifiers," as opposed to their "signifieds" or "referents" – that keep proliferating as print culture expands, shifting across different meanings, and thereby altering perceptions of what their "true" referents are. Of course, the appearance/reality disconnect pervades her relationship with the Prince in the *Memoirs* beyond just her cross-dressing and their reenactments of "Perdita" (now her sobriquet in the press) and "Florizel" (Perdita's lover in *A Winter's Tale*) in their letters carried by intermediaries and the public parodies of their relationship (*WMR* 1: xvii–viii). When, in a 1783 letter included in the "Continuation" (7: 261–267), Robinson recalls her last night on stage before leaving theater for the Prince in May 1780 (1: xxxv), she remembers this final exit as "flying from a happy certainty to pursue the phantom disappointment" (7: 262). The specter of what first promises "visionary happiness" despite her admitted adultery (262) turns Gothically, as she writes, into literal disappointment, the detachment of that envisioned signifier from the referent to which it first seemed appointed, making it only a "phantom." The Prince suddenly dropped her in December 1780 (1: xxxv), and both of them were cast, as she later recounts it, into a terrifying chaos, the pervasive "artillery" of "slander" in "pamphlets . . . paragraphs, and caricatures" (7: 265), all signifiers of other signifiers, just some among the "legion of these phantoms it has been my fate to encounter" (7: 267). That Gothic shift from a singular, exalted object of desire to its explosion into myriad ghost-like falsities on paper ironically echoes, as the *Memoirs* recall it, the author's earlier marriage in 1773 to the solicitor's clerk Thomas Robinson

(1: xxxiii) – whom she never legally divorced – at the behest of her mother to restore the family fortunes. Initially she accepts Hester's image of Thomas as prompting "an impression of gratitude" by "attending" Mary during an illness (7: 209) and claiming to be an "heir" through an uncle to a "handsome fortune" (213). Yet these all dissipate into phantoms when he is revealed to be "the illegitimate son" of that "uncle" (213), a debtor and deceiving adulterer worse than Mary's father (224), and a begrudged hanger-on at that "uncle's" country seat, Tregunter. This mansion, too, first meets the "eye" as the antiquated center of "a romantic space of scenery" (216), yet it turns out to be *faux* Gothic, "not yet finished," and the scene of haughty "insults" toward Mary because she is middle class, even though the "considerable fortune" behind it comes from "trade" and the family cultivates an ignorance so removed from her rich early education (201–202) that she remembers finding "but few sources of amusement for" a cultivated "female mind" (229). The Gothic fronts of both the Prince and Thomas Robinson the "heir," as in romances from Walpole to Radcliffe, are pierced in the *Memoirs* to show themselves undergirded by corruptions, inconsistencies, and fears of "phantoms" that expose one counterfeit identity after another, all disappointments, even in Mary Robinson the actress, wife, and mistress.

The Inescapable Gothic

Ultimately her successful flights from such roles in the 1780s–90s, even her astonishing productivity as a writer over her final decade, do not, as her *Memoirs* recount them, escape the vagaries and fakery of Gothic sensibility. When, after the Prince drops her, she flees from England to France in October 1781 (*WMR* 1: xxxv), she finds herself transported far from the dark slanders of London, lavishly feted as "*la belle Angolise*" (7: 268). She even accepts an invitation from Marie Antoinette and dresses for the occasion in "the fashion of the French Court" (269), yet another counterfeit identity. But, as the *Memoirs*' "Continuation" admits, the Queen particularly notices the "miniature of the Prince of Wales, which Mrs. Robinson wore on her bosom" (269). The distance from England and scandal suddenly collapses, first because Robinson's sensibility obviously still longs for him, but also because this moment recalls the haunting power of portraits in Gothic fictions going back, again, to Walpole's *Otranto*. There Matilda, Manfred's daughter, feels herself attracted to Theodore, apparently a young peasant (Walpole 2003: 76), primarily because he resembles "the picture of the good Alfonso in the gallery" to which she believes "my destiny is linked" (2003: 95). Such a "destiny" is what Robinson keeps having to admit about the Prince in her *Memoirs*, as we see in the 1781 painting of her by Thomas Gainsborough (see Figure 2), where she holds that very miniature, in one of

Figure 2 Thomas Gainsborough, 1781 (oil on canvas), *Mrs. Mary Robinson (Perdita)*, Wallace Collection, London, UK / © Wallace Collection/Bridgeman Images.

several portraits of her (including Figure 1) done at a time when she hovered between celebrated and notorious in the English public eye (Ty 27–28, 38). Later in the *Memoirs*, too, Robinson is Gothically dragged back in other ways. In July 1783, when she starts out for the Continent again, this time in pursuit of lover Banastre Tarlton (*WMR* 1: xxxv–vi), she is figured forth by the "Continuation" as a sentimental and Gothic heroine in a sequence which begins with "her fate assumed darker hue," makes no mention of Tarlton at all, and describes her as "attacked by a malady" from "exposure to the night air" that forces her back to

England and *"progressively deprived her of the use of her limbs"* (7: 270). This is the *Memoirs'* romanticized rendition of Robinson "fall[ing] ill" while traveling, "possibly" from "a miscarriage," into a "fever" that led by 1784 to a "progressive paralysis" that she did indeed "suffer for the remainder of her life" (1: xxxvi).

Even so, this dark descent becomes one of several moments from which she pulls herself up, as from Gothic "melancholy" ashes, to "pour forth . . . poetic effusions" of "genius" and, by the mid-1790s, to become an authority on how "modern poetry [should be] composed," if often from older models (7: 278). For the "Continuation" narrator, in fact, it is the "mournful certainty" of "incurable lameness," somewhat like the "church-yard of Old Windsor" where she asks to be buried (7: 290), that repeatedly gives rise to "the activity of a fertile fancy" (280), recalling her view of such mental expansion as born into her, given her Gothic birthplace. The "Continuation" does acknowledge, as the later Robinson did (*WMR* 1: xix), some regrettable detours motivated by her sentimental inclinations, particularly in 1790. Around that time, as the "Continuation" narrator puts it, she gives in to another counterfeit costume, the "poetical disguise" that is the "extravagance" of the "Della Crusca" school of "Robert Merry," to which Robinson actively contributed poems (*WMR* 7: 279). Still, this brief excrescence (really from 1788–91; 1: xxxvi), as viewed in the *Memoirs*, is left behind by her many publishing triumphs of the later 1790s and her appointment in 1799 to head "the poetical department of a morning paper" (7: 286), *The Morning Post* (1: xxxviii). When the "Continuation" concludes by judging Robinson's life, though, following her daughter's account of her death, the sentimental Gothic keeps enveloping what is written about her. As much as Robinson finally achieved, we are told that her legacy remains haunted by the dark "errors" that often "combined to her destruction" and that her continuous "mental exertions through [her] depressing disease" should "extort admiration," but only as such an "unmitigable severity . . . awaken[s] pity in the hardest heart" (7: 292).

2 The Ungrounded Grounds of the Walpolean Gothic

Even so, when I say that Robinson drives down to, and then draws forth, the very bases of the Walpolean Gothic, I mean that the Gothic in her writing at its best reenacts the most underlying symbolic dynamics of the "Gothic Story" as Walpole first defined them and as they were developed further by his best successors. Just as the *Memoirs'* account of Robinson's birth invokes the "two kinds of romance" in Walpole's second Preface, it also hearkens back to the radical suggestions about the "ancient" kind in his *first* Preface of 1764, nearly always reprinted with the second. In that Preface, where the author claims to be the translator of an Italian text printed in 1529 by an "artful" Catholic trying to counter the Reformation (Walpole 2003: 59), the "preternatural" elements in the story are castigated as relics from the "darkest ages of christianity" that should not be believed in by enlightened Protestant readers (59–60). Nearly all the elements in *Otranto* that assume a supernatural plane and exclusively Catholic beliefs, then, come to the reader with their ideological foundations "exploded now even from romances," even as such symbols emptied of those grounds arouse, as in Burke, pleasurable nostalgia for modern imaginations (60). Hence the oddities in the influential ghosts of *Otranto*, two of them imitative of the Ghost of the Prince's Father in Shakespeare's *Hamlet* (declared as a source in Walpole's second Preface, 66–67). They are all hollowed-out specters compared to Shakespeare's embodied figure, images of other images rather than signifiers of a once-present and solid entity. They are the gigantic ghost of the murdered Alfonso in armored fragments that resembles the statue of him beneath the Otranto "church," also in armor like the *Hamlet* ghost (76); the shade of "the portrait" of Manfred's "grandfather" that "quit[s] its panel" to walk silently across the castle "floor" (81); and the cowled specter that appears to Frederic (156–157) to remind him of an old Hermit who once spoke prophetically to him (133) but that now looks like a skeleton in a *danse macabre* painting of the 1400s. Readers have been told by the first Preface to dismiss the belief-system that credits these apparitions, to see them as hollow memorials of old-style ghosts, and to feel only the sheer "Terror" that the characters do upon beholding them (60). Actual deaths or "ancient" world views that these shades might once have signified have receded so far into the past that such contents are now as absent to our logical understanding as they are felt and dimly desired by our emotions in a Burkean "sublime" reaction. That is precisely how Robinson comes to see the Gothic scene of her birth, with its ruins as towering over her birthplace and as fragmented and divorced from their Catholic base as the ghost of Alfonso is for Walpole's readers. Hence her "melancholy awe," even now, in her *Memoirs*. Such piles arouse a complex emotion combining the loss of that past, only vaguely still desired – hence the melancholy – with the pleasure of that awareness as the worst of those ages recedes in favor of a more modern, Protestant sense of humanity's relationship to signs of a higher divinity – hence the awe.

"Gothic" as Mobile Signifier

Robinson is also a reenactor of other levels among Walpole's peculiar assumptions. For one thing, she accepts, as he does, "Gothic" as a floating signifier. For her as for him, it slides, not just between ancient and modern romance, but between two ideological stances toward its "ancient" connotations that contended with each other in the eighteenth century. One of these, what Dale Townshend terms "dark Gothic," saw the term as meaning "monstrous" and "uncivilized," recalling a medieval antiquity of tyrannical hierarchies, continuous violence, and enslavement by superstition; the other, "white Gothic" (borrowed by Townshend from David Punter), held out to more modern times a "pleasant and anodyne medievalism" – hence the Gothic Revival in eighteenth-century architecture (see also Groom 57–62) – that longed for "fantasies of chivalry, heroism, and splendour" linked vaguely to the "liberty" supposedly achieved by the Magna Carta in 1215, provided the real social foundations of all of these were obscured (Townshend 33–39). Both are there in Walpole's *Otranto*, with Manfred pulled toward the tyrannical and Theodore toward the chivalric, *and* in Robinson's "melancholy awe," which vaguely laments the fragmented wonders of the Bristol Minster while happily seeing its militaristic, aristocratic, and Catholic past in ruins. Robinson also furthers Walpole's use of "Goth" in some of his letters (see Walpole 2016: IV, 699) to refer to contemporaries determined to uphold long-past attitudes for bad *or* good reasons, as in her *Memoirs*' description of her husband's sister as "Gothic in her appearance and stiff in her deportment" (*WMR* 7: 217) but also in one of her novels, where an aristocratic villain's worst tendencies are restrained by "the gothic rules of freedom and humanity" (*WMR* 2: 404).

"Gothic" for Robinson is thus like Walpole's *Otranto* ghosts, a mobile signifier of other signifiers more than any grounded historical referent. That is only fitting for a term that, since the early 1500s, was really a pejorative misnomer used by neo-classicists to criticize medieval pointed-arch buildings that were never built by Goths (Townshend 36). Hence, as a term always distanced from any real origins, Walpole's "Gothic" easily joins forces with Burke's "terror sublime," since the signifiers that provoke the latter in his *Enquiry* are equally removed from any grounded past or death they might signify. When the pieces of the giant ghost of Alfonso come together at the end of *Otranto* to "ascend" toward "the form of St. Nicholas" in a heaven visualized as the ceiling of a Catholic cathedral (Walpole 2003: 162), readers, who should disbelieve in any reality behind such iconography because of the first Preface, should regard such symbols as sublime but empty signifiers. Readers are urged to focus instead on the emotional reactions of the remaining characters, who believe all this only because of the associations of ideas with which their medieval-Catholic educations have imbued their minds. It is in this "modern" psychological, not "ancient" supernatural, scheme that the "walls of the castle" of Otranto being "thrown down" by Alfonso's ascension (162) lead to Robinson's setting her birth in a "gothic structure" that arouses "awe" now because its past groundings recall a fabled past, yet one that is also substantially in ruins. Even more than Walpole, she is placing herself at a point of historical transition into what Charles Taylor has called the more modern and secular "social imaginary"; there the beliefs behind Enlightenment practices and institutions are

becoming more dominant, while older, religion-based alternatives are still drawing adherents, making each ideology "one among many" (Taylor 171, 12) – the
cultural tension, we now see, that gave rise to Gothic fiction.

The Spectrality of Empiricism

At this stage in her *Memoirs*, however, Robinson is also reconstructing 1756–7
and the Bristol Minster-house while she is writing just "north of Piccadilly" in
1798 (see *WMR* 7: 193, 359 n.1). She therefore has to wonder whether what she
is claiming to perceive again could be among the "legion" of "phantoms it has
been [her] fate to encounter." While she often does want to distinguish concep-
tually between perceptions that can be grounded in "truth" and ghost-like
impressions that lead to "the disappointment" of what they promise, nearly
every observation recounted in the *Memoirs* is of the latter kind. "The images
which are" initially "stamped on the brain," the points of departure for sensibility and the association of ideas as Robinson has a character describe them in
a Gothic novel of 1797 (*WMR* 5: 29), are for her quite similar to Walpole's
ungrounded ghosts. They are specters of images pulled away from any clear
base that end up referring more to the feelings about them in their imaginers or
observers than any point of reference outside of perception. Locke, after all, in
establishing empirical association and the roots of sensibility theory in 1690,
declared that every basic perception is indeed an image, impressed on the
mind's *tabula rasa*, that is always already becoming the ghost-like "Shadow"
of a remembered sense perception; indeed, all such "Pictures drawn in our
Minds" for Locke will fast become "Tombs" unless these initial impressions are
"refreshed" by associations with other "ideas" and feelings about them based on
similar imprints (Locke 151–152). Consequently, the characters in *Otranto* see
almost everything as readers see its ghosts: signifying just another signifier that
may hide yet another behind it, as when "the mark of a bloody arrow" on
Theodore's "shoulder" proves him to be the long-lost son of Father Jerome,
a priest who has kept hidden all such signs of his unpriestly past (Walpole 2003:
110–111). In Radcliffe's Gothic romances, too, as Terry Castle has shown,
characters find their perceptions always becoming "subjective, delicately emotional," and "spectral images" that ultimately "reduce" every "other" to "a
phantom," so much so that "nature itself becomes a mere screen" painted in
the mind (Castle 234–245). Robinson, in turn, extends this empirical spectrality
in her *Memoirs*, in which every man she loves is "a phantom" only briefly hiding
eventual "disappointment"; every Gothic cathedral is a recollection of her
birthplace, itself a spectral memory when she writes about it (see Setzer); and
all those she detests are nearly always Gothicized by being spectralized.

She describes "Molly" Edwards, the housekeeper at Tregunter, by claiming that "a more overbearing, vindictive spirit never inhabited the heart of mortal" (*WMR* 7: 216). Robinson may have observed her via empirical perceptions, but she turns these perceptions into ghost-like memory-traces, much as Locke and Radcliffe do, into which, since Robinson cannot see physically inside Molly, she can project her own associations and feelings about certain human traits.

The Gothic as Theater

Meanwhile, this empirical ghostliness looking back to Walpole also comes to Robinson conjoined, as the former actress surely realized, with the unabashed theatricality of Gothic prose narrative. Before his second *Otranto* Preface cites Shakespeare and *Hamlet* as sources, his first one extols his tale as following the "rules of the drama," referring to its characters as "actors" (Walpole 2003: 60). Hence *The Castle of Otranto* has long been (in)famous for its big-stage "spectacle" (2003: 74–76, 117–118), its declamatory dialogue (124–126), and the theatrical posturing of its characters (160–162). It is not just because she has been a theater actress, then, that Robinson's *Memoirs* contain many scenes written in just such a melodramatic manner. Recalling one of her returns to the Bristol cathedral, she clearly stages Walpolean theater: "I heard the . . . long-remembered organ flinging its loud peal through the Gothic Structure. . . . The mouldering walk was gloomy . . . 'Here', said I, 'did my infant feet pace to and fro'" (*WMR* 7: 214). At the same time, though, she records an internal series of thoughts as both worded and yet beyond words: "how little has the misjudging world known of what has passed in my mind, even" in these semi-private "moments of my existence!" (214). Here she hearkens back to Walpole again, but now to those moments of free indirect discourse in *Otranto* when Manfred's thoughts are recorded by the narrator as conflicting with his staged behavior. We are told that he feels "ashamed" of his "inhuman treatment" of Hippolita, for example, and yet that he has "curbed the yearnings of his heart" to make stern speeches to her, "transition[ing] his 'soul . . . to exquisite villainy'" (Walpole 2003: 93) and so playing out a theatrical type at odds with his inner feelings. Walpolean Gothic fiction continually oscillates between dramatic hyperbole and strictly narrative discourse that itself veers between plot transitions and spying on the inner thoughts of characters. Robinson's writing continues this Walpolean aporia. Along with the Janus-faced instability of combining opposed genres (ancient vs. modern), she reworks *Otranto*'s continuous shifting of narrative into drama and vice versa, juxtaposing speeches that seem designed for public theaters with narrated internal struggles intended for private reading.

Readers are left torn, whether they are reading Walpole or Robinson, between how much character in their texts is formed externally by actions, reactions, and directions prescribed by others, since "all the world's a stage" as in Shakespeare, and how much it is generated internally by empirical perceptions and associations of ideas.

This hesitation, inseparable as it is from signs being ghost-like signifiers lacking solid grounds, is what leads to the *in*-distinction of appearance versus apparent reality that bedevils Walpole's *Otranto* and Robinson's *Memoirs*. It is this confusion that best explains the climactic scene in *Otranto* when Manfred, hastening through the dark subterranean passage and believing that the young woman he thinks he sees is the Isabella fleeing from him, tragically "plung[es]" a "dagger... into the bosom" of his daughter, Matilda (Walpole 2003: 158–159). Both young women are written as so similar in appearance, so like the ghost-figures divorced from their different experiences, that it is hard to tell their surfaces apart (as in Walpole 2003: 124, where even Theodore mistakes one for the other). Such ironies are echoed in Robinson's *Memoirs* when her accounts of her father, the Prince of Wales, and Thomas Robinson end up as frightfully similar, despite many deeper differences. They are equally attractive on their signifier-surfaces, and the "phantoms" they present are equally diverted from their anticipated reference points by the "disappointments" that occur when their surfaces are pierced. How can people or characters on their surfaces reveal their distinct depths when their internal and previous lives are obscured by their appearances in an environment where life is theater, yet where such depths really do exist? As an intermediary between Walpole and Robinson, even Radcliffe has left the Gothic caught in this quandary within its basic dynamics. When her *Italian* introduces the "physiognomy" of Schedoni, it is drawing on a quasi-science made famous two decades earlier by Johann Caspar Lavatar (see *WMR* 4: 281–282 n.32). There the features of the face and skull can be read as a text revealing the inner tendencies of a person, an approach to characterization adopted by several Gothic novelists of the 1790s (see Sedgwick). But the actual description of Schedoni using this scheme reveals "the traces of many passions, which seem to have fixed the features they no longer animated" (Radcliffe 1998*a*: 35). Radcliffe's deceiving monk is like an *Otranto* ghost, the presenter of a surface from which the original grounds have been removed. Consequently, his face can hint both at some "hideous crime in the past" and at his concealment of it "under the disguise of his manners" (1998*a*: 34). Physiognomy simultaneously invites and prevents an observer's attempt to penetrate a surface while it also suggests the very human depth that this surface intimates but can also hide. Robinson's *Memoirs* are captivated by this Gothic conundrum, among so many others. When Robinson recalls playwright and theater-owner Richard Brinsley

Sheridan, she describes him as so "beautifully Sympathetic" to her as an actress that he used his gaze "as if dictated by a superior power" (like Garrick's) to warn her away from would-be lovers because he just knew "that I was *destined to be deceived*" (*WMR* 7: 252). At the same time, she remembers that the "*powerful interest that Mr. Sheridan possessed over my mind*" also gave her "*excessive inquietude*" that he may have had, though he never said so, the same "*perilous...fascination*" with her himself that he warned her against in others (252). Behind one appearance is yet another that can be read in conflicting ways, a warning about deception that may be itself deceptive (like Schedoni), and each appearance can be revealing and opaque at the same time – and hence best described by the Gothic in a Walpolean and Radcliffean way.

The Ghost of the Counterfeit

Indeed, I would go a step further. Robinson's embrace of the Walpole brand of Gothic pulls her into an aesthetic where signifiers not only refer to other signifiers but also to *counterfeit* ones that claim to offer some real object but are deceptively distanced from one. All the *Otranto* ghosts-of-art-objects share this quality, as I have argued elsewhere (see Hogle 1994), and the "phantoms" that are Robinson's Lockean perceptions, particularly of men, ultimately refer to the "disappointment" *in* each phantom's referent that turns (or is likely to turn) that object into a distortion, a faking at best, of what the initial signifier seemed to promise. For Robinson as well as Walpole, this particular dynamic underwrites all the others in the Gothic, from its peculiar mixture of ancient and modern *and* drama and narrative to the history of the term "Gothic." All of these, as we have seen, can make signifiers point initially toward one apparent referent ("Gothic" as recalling the ancient Goths of northern Europe, for example) and can then turn that referent into a counterfeit of it in a different register ("Gothic" as referring to a 1500s misnaming of pointed-arch buildings). As it happens, this underpinning of the Walpolean Gothic stems from its references back to signifiers in Shakespeare and especially *Hamlet*. Even though, as I have noted, two of the disembodied ghosts in *Otranto* allude to the embodied Ghost of Hamlet's Father, the final appearance of that figure in Shakespeare's play comes after the Prince has urged his remarried mother to compare "pictures." He shows her the "counterfeit presentiment of two brothers," one depicting the "grace" on the physiognomy of her dead husband, the poisoned King now a ghost, and the other revealing his brother and her current spouse to be "mildewed" by comparison, a fake king in Hamlet's view and a secret poisoner, as Manfred's grandfather is revealed to be (*Hamlet* III.iv.54–64; Shakespeare 1168). While "counterfeit," on one level here, seems apt for describing only the second picture, that word is used to refer to *both* portraits and so oscillates between meaning a true representation and a deceptive representation of a false substitute. Jean Baudrillard has shown us that "counterfeit" in English at Shakespeare's time did in fact hesitate between these two meanings, one a pictorial "nostalgia for natural reference" in which "assignation [particularly to a class] is absolute" and the other a "transit" of "signs of prestige from one class to another" (like the inferior brother's assumption of King Hamlet's crown); this multiplicity helped facilitate the efforts of the rising middle class at the time to assume the coats of arms and status of near-aristocrats, as Shakespeare did, because aristocracy could be counterfeited by payments for the appropriation of its signifiers (Baudrillard 50–51). The *Otranto* ghosts-of-signifiers, as well as Radcliffe's Schedoni, look back to this Renaissance-era slippage, and so I have termed all such figures "ghosts of the counterfeit" (Hogle 1994: 29–33), in which the "counterfeit" is understood as itself Janus-faced, particularly in Shakespeare's time. It is the earlier signifier (like *Hamlet* for Walpole) that combined a nostalgia for grounded medieval reference points (the original "Amloth" stories being that old; Shakespeare 1136) with the prospect that such nostalgic signs could be shifted from those grounds and appropriated for more modern, class-climbing purposes. For Robinson as much as Walpole, this is precisely the aesthetic tug-of-war, representing and modernizing Shakespeare – which Robinson did many times as an actress in adaptations of him, *Hamlet* included (*WMR* 1: xxxiv–xxxv) – that should be employed by the Gothic when it takes "ancient" icons even more emptied out and refills and juxtaposes them with more current schemes of signification (including empiricism and sentimentality) to address the conditions and audiences of the later 1700s.

There is also another dimension in the Gothic's ghosting of the counterfeit crucial to Robinson's employment of it. When Hamlet looks to the "counterfeit" of his father, he does so after having already wondered if the Ghost has told him the truth about his uncle poisoning his father in Act I. This is the reason, he says in Act II, that he needs "grounds/More relative" to move against his uncle, because the "spirit I have seen"/May be a [dev'l] and the [dev'l] hath power/T'assume "a pleasing shape" (*Hamlet* II.ii.598–604; Shakespeare 1159). This famous doubt comes from Hamlet being pulled from the start between opposed ideologies, one of which is more ancient and one more modern. The moment he first sees the Ghost, he asks whether it is "a spirit of health, or goblin damn'd [?]" (I.iv.40; Shakespeare 1148). He is torn, like his English audience of 1600–01, between a waning and now-suspect Catholic view that ghosts are bearers of genuine revelations (counterfeits as true likenesses) and the emergent Protestant insistence that ghosts are either psychological delusions or agents from Hell (counterfeits as deceptions) trying to ensnare the unwary into sin (see Frye 11–29; see also Groom 41). The principal specter in *Hamlet*, then, is a manifestation of an unresolved ideological quandary simmering in the cultural unconscious of Shakespeare's culture. To look back to such counterfeits, hollowed out of their once-supposed reality while signifying Janus-faced conflicts deep in their milieux, is for the Walpolean Gothic "ghost of the counterfeit" to use those symbols to deal with its own era's conflicts between fading and rising beliefs.

It is on this basis that E. J. Clery rightly sees *The Castle of Otranto* as figuring forth in a suggestive disguise the cultural "contradiction" in 1760s Britain "between the traditional claims of landed property and the new claims of the private family" (Clery 1995: 77). As Clery says, there is a pull in *Otranto* toward aristocratic assumptions with their old Catholic accoutrements and beliefs, whose validity "was symbolically diminished" by 1764 (hence Walpole's ghosts of mere art-objects) and a countering pull, in character behaviors and dialogue like those in the emerging middle-class novel, that "presupposes" the "perspective of bourgeois capitalism" (1995: 73–76). In *Otranto*'s "fictitious will" counterfeiting aristocratic ancestry, such a tug-of-war is also linked in 1764–5 to "contemporary debates on authenticity and forgery" arising from several causes: among them, *faux* Gothic structures (such as Walpole's Strawberry Hill), uncertainties about the "legitimacy" of England's now-German monarchs, and the fakery in the "found [medieval] manuscripts" of James Macpherson and Thomas Chatterton (Croom 71–75). All of this looks back to the spectral manifestations in *Hamlet* of Catholic contending with Protestant beliefs, with the latter turning the former into fictions empty of truth while simultaneously helping to question the legitimacy of a royal succession. Robinson, in building on this legacy of Walpole reworking Shakespeare and Radcliffe and others reworking both, manifests in her *Memoirs* – and, as I now hope to show, in many other works – how the Walpolean Gothic with this history, and because of its contradictory foundations, can draw up for readers and audiences, even while masking, the most unresolved conflicts among ideologies *and* the falsifications produced by those tensions that underlay her life, her era, and her world as she knew it.

3 The Argument

Indeed, it is in Mary Darby Robinson's use of the Walpolean Gothic, especially its foundational contradictions, to suggest underlying cultural quandaries and their effects on dispossessed people – usually women, but others as well – that she, I would argue, achieves her truly distinctive contribution to the Gothic mode across the 1790s. Granted, this development was not immediate in her writing. It might seem in her poems, from her early ones published in 1775 to her later collections through 1796, that Robinson does employ imagery that could be seen as "Gothic." In "Letter to a Friend on Leaving Town" (1775; *WMR* 1: 22–24), for instance, her speaker makes "the inchanting shades of gay Vauxhall" ominously dark (l. 10) and fills this romanticized space with numerous specters of "fashionable vice" all grimly turning into figures of "ruin" (ll. 40–50) as they slide toward "death" (l. 64). In the peak poem of Robinson's Della Cruscan period, "Ainsi va le Monde" addressed to Merry ("So Goes the World," 1790; *WMR* 1: 77–84), "Laura Maria" (one of her many role-plays in poetry) sees her addressee's stylized yet "native Genius" rising like the sun while, she hopes, "The gothic phantoms sick'ning fade away" (ll. 71–72). These phantoms include the pre-Revolutionary France that could "hide pale Slav'ry in a mask of smiles" (l. 201) but also the Revolution's revival of old-style imprisonment in the "black Bastille," where "deep mysterious whispers . . . and death stalked sullen o'er the treacherous ground" (ll. 237–238). Nonetheless, while Walpolean elements do begin to appear, fleetingly, in some Robinson poems prior to 1796, Judith Pascoe is right to find that the sepulchral moments in Robinson's poetry up to that time were seeded most by the "so-called graveyard poets of the mid-eighteenth century" from "Edward Young, author of *Night Thoughts* [1742–5]" to "Robert Blair, author of *The Grave* [1743–7]" (Robinson 2000: 45–48). They, in turn, were influenced by John Milton's "Il Penseroso" and were influential on the settings of Walpole, but their writings, even though they advance a Protestant "awe" that lends new significance to Catholic tombs, participate only some in the contradictions of the "Gothic Story" that became increasingly important to Robinson as the 1790s progressed. For me it is in her final poems after 1796, especially several that she gathered in her *Lyrical Tales* just before she died, where the Walpolean mode that she has explored until then, primarily in prose fiction, enters her verse in the most powerful coalescence she ever achieved of the Gothic and poetry.

Before that point, the clearest sign of the Walpolean Gothic coming into Robinson's writing is the publication in 1792, following the meteoric success of Radcliffe's *The Romance of the Forest* (1791), of her insistently Gothic novel *Vancenza*, although its allusions to Radcliffe are mostly to *A Sicilian Romance* (*WMR* 2: 438 n.3). As William D. Brewer and Robinson's *Memoirs* tell us, "the initial print run sold out in a single day," because of both the Gothic's burgeoning popularity and "Perdita's notoriety" (*WMR* 1: xx–xxi). Understandably, Robinson saw such writing, in addition to its symbolic suggestiveness (much of which she did use to parallel her life), as a way to make the money she desperately needed, in part because a legacy promised by the Prince was only sporadically and never fully paid (*WMR* 1: xviii). Consequently, with astonishing dedication given her fragile health, she produced a rapid succession of

Gothic works after *Vancenza,* predominantly novels: *The Widow* (1794), *Angelina* (1796), *The Sicilian Lover* (an unproduced play printed in 1796), *Hubert de Sevrac* (late 1796), *Walsingham* (late 1797), *The False Friend* (1799), and *The Natural Daughter* (also 1799), this last only intermittently Gothic, all of which immersed her in the Walpolean "blend" of genres that she quite understandably continued in her *Memoirs.* To be sure, these works, except at certain moments (see below), do not attain Radcliffe's level of artistic quality. Robinson admitted as much near the end of her life. "Most of her writings," Maria records her dying mother saying near the end of the *Memoirs,* were "composed in too much haste" out of financial necessity (*WMR* 7: 290). Consequently, plot-patterns and character-types are repeated from work to work, particularly heroines suspected of more sexual sins than they have really committed, with the side-plot of *Angelina,* in particular, being only a slightly different version of the main plot in *The Widow* (*WMR* 3: ix). Robinson also, probably to gain more volumes and sales, inserts some long segments of mostly non-Gothic comedy (as in *Walsingham* [*WMR* 5: 153–160, 293–297]) that echo her own unsuccessful attempt at onstage satire in a play, *Nobody* (1794), targeted at the upper classes and their gambling habits (*WMR* 1: xxi; WMR 8: 23–50). She even dots several of these novels, as Ann Radcliffe does in hers, with inserted poems, most of them ostensibly written by central characters (e.g., in *The Widow* [*WMR* 2: 375–376, 468] and in *Walsingham* [*WMR* 5: 20, 137–138, 355]) that advance the echoes of graveyard, elegiac, neo-classical, and sentimental verse in her earlier work without alluding specifically to the Walpolean Gothic – though perhaps a little in "The Doublet of Grey" in *Walsingham* (*WMR* 5: 300–303) – except by echoing this mingling of genres in Radcliffe's romances.

Even so, in such bastings-together of literary modes calculated for popularity and admittedly derivative to start with, Robinson does achieve powerful symbolic resonances within her adaptations of Walpolean schemes by reworking certain Gothic motifs repeatedly across multiple episodes while she is drawing readers and characters toward the scenic features – the old edifices, underground vaults, hidden chambers, and sequestered manuscripts – that we see in *Otranto* and every Radcliffe romance. It is such motifs, as each recurs across her novels and gathers complications as it develops, that I propose to analyze in the sections that follow before examining how she extends Gothic further in exemplary *Lyrical Tales.* All of these reveal in their different ways underlying psychological and cultural quandaries, the deep-seated contestations of contending belief-systems in the Western personal *and* cultural unconscious of the 1790s, which the Walpolean Gothic is especially suited to articulate, as well as disguise, by being an unsettling, Janus-faced mixture of genres and styles that itself looks back to the conflicts among beliefs and discourses in the counterfeits of Shakespeare's time.

True, it can be argued that Robinson's novels frequently depart from Walpolean precedents because five of the seven are epistolary, written as successions of letters posted and answered, except for *Walsingham* with its long first-person narrative enclosed in letters that frame it. Each of these unquestionably recalls Samuel Richardson's *Pamela* (1740) and *Clarissa* (1747–8), Jean-Jacques Rousseau's *Julie; or the New Eloise* (1762), and J.W. von Goethe's *The Sorrows of Young Werther* (1774), all well known to Robinson as landmarks in the literature of sensibility. This choice allows her characters to vent their internal debates and to recount action and emotion from their biased perspectives, letting readers into their closets (the place where most silent reading occurred) and opening out the revelations of unspoken thought previously consigned to indirect-discourse moments in Walpole, Radcliffe, and others. Across Robinson's writing, in fact, this further blurring of generic boundaries, in addition to facilitating her desire to appeal to many audiences, augments the capacity of the sentimental Gothic to juxtapose conflicting modes of discourse and their competing ideologies. For Robinson, even more than Walpole or Radcliffe, the Gothic becomes a form of what Jean-François Lyotard has called a "*différend*," "a case of conflict" where "judgments" about any subject are suspended "between heterogenous genres" and their opposed points of view (Lyotard ix). The Gothic as *différend* is what allows her major characters, like the author herself, to manifest their dispossession in worlds torn between antiquated and revolutionary understandings that pull them in multiple directions at once, as readers of Mary Robinson are still pulled today.

4 The Gothic Image of the Defining Other

Vancenza (1792)

Among the motifs in Robinson's novels that are the most repeated *and* ideologically divided, one that is foregrounded quite often in her earliest Gothics, as well as later ones, recalls the fascination with the ancestral portrait in *The Castle of Otranto*. In *Vancenza*, Elvira, the orphan taken into Castle Vancenza in fifteenth-century Spain – echoing Charlotte Smith's *Emmeline, the Orphan of the Castle* (1788; *WMR* 2: 441 n. 34) – falls in love with the young Prince Almanza from a nearby principality. She is soon "assailed" in her dreams by "the image of the Prince," recalling Matilda's *Otranto* fixation on the picture of Alfonso, and by that image "present[ing]" her an additional "portrait of a lady holding in her hand a bleeding heart" that looks exactly like her; her uncertain status makes marriage to this Prince forbidden, after all, under the age-old codes of aristocratic rank, so she deposits her "fatal secret in the hidden recesses of her heart" (*WMR* 2: 264) with a mindset that "blends all its faculties with those of a dear *second self*" (2: 287, Robinson's italics). Despite warnings she hears against excess sensibility, she maintains this fixation even after seeing mysterious "characters" engraved on "pieces of glass" in a "gallery" at Vancenza that intimate "mouldering reliques" nearby (2: 275). This Gothic setting has hidden within it "a hollow space" containing a "small casket" behind yet another ancestral portrait, this one of Madeline Vancenza, the dead sister of the current Count and Elvira's actual mother (2: 328–329). That image hearkens back to the mother of Julia in Radcliffe's *Sicilian Romance*, the true "marchioness" of Mazzini, who has been immured alive and resembles Julia's mental image of her sister, Emilia, and a "miniature" of the marchioness discovered at Castle Mazzini (Radcliffe 1993: 174, 27). The Vancenza casket, however, also contains an anguished account (like the "authentic writing" at the end of *Otranto*) confessing Madeline's attraction to the seemingly "benevolent surface" of the elder Prince Almanza, who "triumphed over her lost honor" and left her pregnant with the current Prince; the latter is thus revealed to be the *brother* of Elvira, who now turns out to have been obsessed with the image of an incestuous love-object even more forbidden to her than before (*WMR* 2: 331–333). Elvira, her entire sense of being of shattered by this reversal, sinks "*into the arms of death*" (2: 337), albeit beatifically like Richardson's Clarissa.

    Vancenza's surface suggestion that all of this could have been avoided, as in its subtitle (*The Dangers of Credulity*), is really belied by its Gothic and sentimental elements and how they enforce women's *un*avoidable entrapment in Janus-faced contradictions built into the ideological schemes that control their thinking. Walpole's Matilda, in obsessing over Theodore's resemblance to Alfonso, is at least linking her "destiny," if unknowingly, to the actual heir to Otranto. Elvira, while similarly tying her existence to her image of Prince Almanza, is more explicitly making that phantom other her "*second self*," an ancestor of what would become various kinds of Gothic doubles in the nineteenth century. Such a figure gives the self, heretofore lacking definition, its first sense of coherence by reflecting its possibilities back to her, raising her above uncertain inconsistencies, especially if that figure, ideologically, is the ultimate male mirror (a Prince, the dream-other of every Cinderella). In the belief-systems that govern her thoughts – and thereby "assail" her from outside her – Elvira cannot conceive of herself to *be* without this male image, even when she is warned against deceptive men by the same beliefs. This conflict within her ideologies is inherent in the Gothic portrait-image as always the specter of a counterfeit to some degree (with Elvira's vision of Almanza recalling the Lockean ghost of her easily deceived first impressions of him) and in the philosophy of sensibility, where the outpouring of love by a woman, supposedly the greatest fulfillment of her, always risks the excesses, self-punishment, and shame to come if it is unrequited or misplaced (as in the dream-image of the Almanza-image handing Elvira a companion-image of herself in another portrait-mirror where she holds her naked heart).

These paradoxes are endemic in the world of this novel, not just as products of the ideologies at the time it appeared, but as proclivities inherited from birth, also ideological constructs. In the manuscript left by Elvira's mother, as Stephanie Ross has said, Robinson employs the "trope of maternal transmission ... common in eighteenth-century literature," in this case so that a "mother's sexual transgressions" clearly have "consequences" that "reverberate into a second generation" (Ross 67). The adulterous woman who supplanted the sequestered mother in *A Sicilian Romance* (Radcliffe 1993: 176) is transferred into the signifiers of the absent mother herself in *Vancenza*. The double bind of sensibility, loving sincerely yet frequently being deceived, is now a haunting inheritance transmitted through ghostly counterfeits instead of just a recent occurrence. This whole maternal past is what reappears both in the portrait and on the medieval glass of the Vancenza gallery. For Robinson these are woven into the ancient fabric of this novel's Gothic backdrop, but they also draw Elvira and readers toward what has become a "hollow space" at the gallery's real center. It is now filled in retrospectively with a more modern belief about excess sensibility, here recast as a kind of inherited predestination. It is that newer ideology counterfeited as ancient that now "assails" young women with a sense of an apparent "fatal" destiny coming out of the familial past, because of which they believe they do not have the choice of avoiding the male image/portrait that can seem their defining second self.

The False Friend (1799)

This Gothic motif, moreover, reappears seven years later in Robinson's *The False Friend*, and here the revelations about female entrapment become even starker. While *Vancenza* does invoke one aspect of Matilda's *Otranto* fixation on Alfonso's picture, it sidesteps another implication: that the young woman's attraction is really to the ultimate patriarch, the founder of Otranto, far more significant for her "destiny" than her biological parents. The characters in *Otranto* are really looking to the ultimate Father, be He God or St. Nicholas or Alfonso in his final "magnitude" (Walpole 2003: 162), to be the insurer of some stable "truth," if only as an image up in Heaven. All those involved, including Walpole and his readers, desire some reliable continuity of ongoing grounds, especially in the transition from "ancient" to "modern." Hence, so that all grounding does not seem lost, the underwriter of woman's fixation on the male portrait is still the idea of the Patriarch as the looming image behind all images, the ultra-Gothic figure (always counterfeited in *Otranto*) who is willingly accepted – particularly by women – as reappearing in Theodore's face. It is to the power of that ideological construct that women are still subjected, even when they seem released from victimization by men. It is this side of the *Otranto* male image that Robinson takes up and Gothically reveals as relentlessly destructive by bringing out *its* contradictions in *The False Friend*.

This novel's heroine, Gertrude St. Leger, like Elvira initially called an "orphan" (*WMR* 6: 3), encounters multiple "friends" whose appearances turn out to be "phantoms" of counterfeits. But *The False Friend* title ultimately fits the ambiguous Lord Denmore the most. He is the appointed guardian-aristocrat to whose castle Gertrude is sent because he was the best friend of her supposedly dead father, William St. Leger, whose "portrait" she wears around her neck despite the "senseless lineaments of that countenance" (6: 47), another specter from which all life and history have been withdrawn. From the moment she meets Denmore, though he has a physiognomy more "sallow than animated" and thus suggests some life drained from his visage too (15), Gertrude becomes as transfixed as Walpole's Matilda is: "The image of Lord Denmore," she writes to *her* best friend, soon "was too deeply impressed upon my imagination, to be effaced by any mortal event" (85). She is so subjected to his gaze and thus so enamored of him that "when I meet [his] dark and penetrating eyes," recalling those of Radcliffe's Schedoni, "I become as it were *nothing*" (86). Similarly, the bust of Denmore (reminiscent of Alfonso's sculpted statue) in his castle's archaic library, as Gertrude views it, "seems" in its stare "to possess the powers of the basilisk" over her (46). For the ancient Greeks that look is the petrifying or deadly gaze of a serpent king (*WMR* 6: 413 n.58), and Gertrude carries that mythology on even though, echoing the first *Otranto* Preface, she soon withdraws this ancient belief from that bust by lamenting her state of mind "when superstition rules it" (46). In this case, though, this imposing image of the other gazing back is not that of a very old male ancestor passed down to a distant descendant. It turns out that, behind his inconsistent reactions to his ward from stern command to bursts of affection, lies the eventual revelation – confessed by Denmore to his fiancée, Miss Stanley, and confirmed by a once-"mysterious paper" (again like the "authentic writing" of *Otranto*) – that Lord Denmore has always been Gertrude's biological father (407).

The supposed dead father, St. Leger, has been a counterfeit in his lifeless portrait, since he finally reveals himself as actually alive (404), and has thus covered up the paternity of the "sallow," half-dead Denmore, who has himself piled on layers of falsity. Both men are echoes of the *Otranto* ghosts, spectral figures who are disappointing, divorced from the meanings that Gertrude has originally assigned them. Denmore has seduced and impregnated his best friend's wife in India and long concealed his own adultery and that of Gertrude's mother, partly because of the latter's deathbed plea that he do so (407–408). The result is his conflicted physiognomy fearful of "being unmasked" as "the destroyer of the original Gertrude St. Leger" and the father of her illegitimate namesake (Brewer 2011: 790–791), who, like Theodore recalling Alfonso, looks just like her mother and so has seemed to be her ghost to Lord Denmore (*WMR* 7: 407). Robinson has significantly contorted Denmore's resemblance to Radcliffe's Schedoni. In *The Italian* that calculating monk sneaks up on the sleeping Ellena di Rosalba to stab her, only to stop when he sees the miniature she wears that suggests he is her father (Radcliffe 1998*a*: 234–236), and that impression ends up exposed as itself a false appearance, like Schedoni's physiognomy, when the real father, though seen only in a picture, turns out to be his nobler and murdered older brother (1998*a*: 381–382). The Schedoni-esque Denmore is the biological father that Schedoni is not, and yet he retains and augments many of the latter's layers of villainous counterfeiting, ending up more a repellant palimpsest than a grounding reference point, since he, unlike Walpole's Alfonso, willfully conceals his fatherhood from the moment Gertrude the mother reveals her pregnancy. There really is no authentic ground in the end behind all these figures of figures for the dominant image and gaze of the male in *The False Friend*. Even so, the daughter Gertrude, along with others, accepts the image of Denmore's gaze as the defining vision of her, even after her Lord's counterfeitings have been revealed. Like Elvira, Gertrude finds the chief mirror of her being to be only a signifier of even more falsifying signifiers, and she dies, once she knows that, in the castle graveyard to be "deposited" there in the "monument" of the "family" that looms up imposingly under the name "Denmore" (*WMR* 6: 408). On one level, she *is* finally "nothing" apart from her incorporation into the patriarchal order, hollowed out as it is, especially when her tomb comes under the gaze of anyone still living. The "ancient" assurance attached to the name of the Father may be more of a ghost of falsity upon falsity in this novel than it is in *Otranto*, but the sheer signifying name of the main father figure nevertheless continues to underwrite the power of the male image and the capacity of its gaze to seem the source of meaning and value for women.

To be sure, as the inherently conflicted Gothic encourages, there is a modernizing countermovement in *The False Friend*, an ideological valuing up of women for several potentials in them: their endurance across generations despite male domination, their self-control if and when they achieve real independence (mentally, as well as socially), and their capacities for high art and how these can return from repression the powers of self-representation stirring in women since ancient times. Though Gertrude, like Elvira, inherits a history of maternal adultery which she herself does not (but is rumored to) duplicate, she also, echoing Walpole's Theodore, repeats the face of the elder Gertrude so exactly that she haunts her guardian with her mother's virtues; the coolheaded Miss Stanley, particularly after she breaks her engagement to Denmore, becomes the reliable and independent reconstructor of history in the novel's final letters (*WMR* 6: 406–408); and the old library at Castle Denmore contains, alongside the owner's "bust," a sculpted "Grecian Sappho," a marble tribute to a "Genius" who "seize[s] upon [Gertrude's] imagination" as if by osmosis (6: 45, 50–51). Sappho is, of course, the ancient singer thought to be *the* first woman poet whose persona Robinson has often assumed by this time, particularly in her 1796 sonnet cycle, *Sappho and Phaon* (*WMR* 1: 320–344), which most firmly established her among English literati as the "English Sappho" (1: xvii–xix), a woman with literary power of her own who, like Gertrude potentially, both reincarnates and modernizes an age-old exemplar. It is really not surprising that *The False Friend* goes this far, since, one month later in 1799, Robinson published, under the name Anne Frances Randall, *A Letter to the Women of England, on the Injustice of Mental Subordination* (*WMR* 8: 129–164). This pamphlet was, by its own admission (8: 131), an extension of the argument in Wollstonecraft's *Vindication* two years after that author's death in 1797 (*WMR* 1: xxi–xxii; 8: xvii–xviii). Even so, when the *Letter* calls on women to "subdue that prejudice," that acceptance of male domination in their minds "which has, for ages past, been your inveterate enemy" like a persistent paternal specter (8: 159), it is building on *The False Friend* almost as much as the *Vindication*.

Nonetheless, "Gertrude's patriarchal burden," which we now see as rooted in the Walpolean Gothic image of the primal Father, finally "obliterate[s] any positive influence Sappho might have had on her" (Brewer 2011: 795). Right after she first sees that bust, she thinks of that largely unknown native of Lesbos as being "the victim of a hopeless passion" (*WMR* 6: 51). Gertrude, like Robinson in her sonnets, reconstructs that ancient singer's history as it appears in Ovid's verse epistle *Sappho to Phaon* and Alexander Pope's 1712 translation of it, in which Sappho passionately seeks the loving gaze of her male boatman as essential to her being and, faced with his rejection, throws herself into the sea (Brewer 2011: 792). Sappho as presented in *The False Friend,* then – known exclusively, even for Robinson, only through male accounts and questionable translations of her – was as mentally arrested by the defining male image as Gertrude is, although we know that Robinson herself "resented what she regarded as [Ovid's] and Pope's disparagement of a poet whom she considered

to be a poetic forebear" (Brewer 2011: 793). Like women in the philosophy of
sensibility, Sappho as an exemplary female is both valued highly as a native
genius and put in question as too emotional. This ideological and psychological
conundrum is never resolved in *The False Friend,* and so it becomes a major
dynamic played out in this novel's most Gothic scenes. When Gertrude moves
the library busts to her own castle chamber, her "gloomy fancies" lure her into
"gazing intently on the bust of my dear . . . guardian," to a point where she both
"presse[s] the cold marble to my burning lips," as though it were a Walpolean
specter coming to life, and beholds the "eyes . . . fixed in a cold and ghastly
sameness" that "reminded me of death" (*WMR* 6: 360). This metamorphosis of
her defining image reveals how much her imagination and its assumptions are
what allow it to still seem alive but also how much it is an antiquated image
emptied of life, as in *Otranto* and its first Preface. This paradox deepens even
more when Gertrude tries "removing" the Denmore bust to her bedroom; in
doing so, she "touched[s]" the Sappho bust, and it falls "to the ground, 'shattered into a thousand pieces'" (360). Gertrude's first reaction is her worry about
the broken figure's effect on Lord Denmore, for whom the "bust was much
valued" because, she finds out only later, it is another image of her dead mother
(374). At no point, even this late when she is faced with a ghostly sculpture in
fragments (like Walpole's Alfonso), does Gertrude see herself as free of self-
subjection to the image and gaze of her Lord, and the consequences dissipate the
possibilities sculpted in the image of both her actual mother and the Founding
Female Poet. Even when the male image exposes the Walpolean emptiness of its
sepulchral visage and the filling of that vacancy by a modern mind too
enthralled by old assumptions, Gertrude's (and Robinson's) need to hold on to
that image as the ground of the self remains so great that it can shatter the
potential for women, briefly visible in Miss Stanley, to achieve independent
power by recovering the fuller history of their female ancestors now available
only in fragments.

Walsingham (1797)

This contradictory power in the defining portrait, however, is not confined for
Robinson to the female obsession with the male image. In *Walsingham*, published
between *Vancenza* and *The False Friend*, she Gothically stages a male obsession
with a female image to the point of intimating deep-seated tensions even more
paradoxical than the ones in these other novels. As a child, Walsingham
Ainsforth, the primary narrator, adopted into the "manor-house of Glenowen"
in Wales (*WMR* 5: 13) somewhat like Elvira and Gertrude, assumes the great
expectations of being the heir to this estate (5: 21). But then his aunt, Lady

Aubrey, removing herself from Glenowen and leaving Walsingham behind, gives birth to a child and announces in a letter – deceptively, it turns out – that the infant is a boy, soon called "Sir Sidney" to emphasize that "he" is now the heir, whereupon Walsingham, with his own excess sensibility (reminiscent of Henry Mackenzie's *The Man of Feeling* [1771; *WMR* 5: xii] as well as Robinson's earlier heroines) "conjure[s] up a thousand phantoms to intimidate my soul" (5: 28). Thus seeing himself Gothically as dispossessed and in need of some new ground to anchor his uprooted identity, he fastens on a succession of images as he grows that he hopes will define him: on the portrait of his dead uncle, whose "eyes appeared to follow me," recalling the picture of Manfred's grandfather in *Otranto* (31); on his remembered first sighting of the adolescent Sir Sidney, at once his most enthralling ("beautiful!") and most abhorred other, "dressed in a vest and pantaloons of blue silk" (53) like *The Blue Boy* (1770; Figure 3) of the Thomas Gainsborough who later painted Robinson; and, so that Walsingham can suppress

Figure 3 Thomas Gainsborough, 1770 (oil on canvas), *The Blue Boy.*
© Courtesy of the Huntington Art Museum, San Marino, California, USA.

his attraction to that image, on his mental picture of Isabella Hanbury, his tutor's sister, who becomes "the object of my enthusiastic idolatry" even when he is away from her (*WMR* 5: 93). With her brother promoting the idea that she is Walsingham's intended, he so fixates on her image as his destiny that he sees a "strong resemblance" to her in the faces of his London landlady, Mrs. Wofford, and her daughter, Amelia, who (he soon realizes) has fallen for him, the object of *her* idolatry (235–237).

This image of another image becomes even more Gothic when Walsingham sees Amelia dressed in a Welsh costume that Isabella once wore: "As she came into the room I started as through I had seen a specter . . . the exact counterpart of Isabella" (5: 244). Simultaneously, he fixates on rumors that Isabella herself is attending balls in a mask to hide the reality that she has become the lover of Sir Sidney, at which Walsingham predictably rages "in an agony of frenzy" (259). Reeling mentally in a hall of mirrors where Gothicized ghosts of counterfeits only reflect others, he kidnaps a masked woman he thinks is Isabella at an Opera House masquerade and takes her to his dark Pall Mall lodgings. There, as this woman barely wakes from having fainted and "hid[es] her face on my shoulder" – while "the image of Isabella still predominate[s]" in his consciousness – "all the laws of honor were violated" by Walsingham's own admission (albeit in a use of passive voice that makes him less of an active agent), even as he blames the "inordinate quantity of wine" he has "swallowed" alongside "my rage and vexation" (265). The next morning, he realizes he has raped "unfortunate Amelia," who has dressed in another one of Isabella's costumes, not the woman he wanted to embrace behind this image. He emphatically castigates himself as a Gothic "villain" (having carried out a threat to Radcliffe heroines that is never actually forced on them) while simultaneously falling back for "extenuation," not just on liquor and passion, but the "capricious[ness]" (he imagines) of "Isabella's conduct" and how "credulous," deceptive, and "fond" Amelia has been (266) – a gesture toward implied consent, weak but still attempted, amid a chaos of inconsistent standards for judging sexual morality.

This episode is, of course, Robinson's most extreme example of the problems with the image of the defining other in her Gothic texts. Moreover, when we realize just how fundamentally Gothic this rape scene is, the contradictions in it and *Walsingham* deepen even more. Granted, to begin with, given the hero's inability to distinguish between two women, this moment echoes Manfred's dimly lit and phallic stabbing of Matilda thinking her to be *another* Isabella in *The Castle of Otranto*. But Robinson's scene goes further by invoking Walpole's equally foundational Gothic play, *The Mysterious Mother*, printed privately in 1768 and never staged in its author's lifetime, but circulated widely enough to influence many of the Gothic tragedies of the 1790s (Walpole 2003: 25–29), including Robinson's *Sicilian Lover* (*WMR* 8: xiii–iv, 51–118). In Walpole's drama, pressured by Catholic priests to reveal long-hidden secrets that may help them deceptively appropriate her castle, the Countess of Narbonne finds her resolve weakening when she beholds her son, Edmund, returned from a distant war and cries: "Art thou my husband … from other orbs/ … Impress'd with every feature I adore …?" (Walpole 2003: 217; III.iii.124–127). She fears Edmund falling in love with her ward, Adeliza, repeating his liaison with a different girl that she strove to interdict years ago on the very day when her husband was bought "before" her "a bloody corse" (2003: 246; V.vi.47–49). Amid her "storm of disappointed passions" that day (as in Walsingham's mental hall of mirrors), the Countess finally has to confess, "Love dress'd [her husband's] image to my longing thoughts" even after his death, and, when she put herself in the place of Edmund's "damsel" in the dark, "my fancy saw thee [Edmund]/Thy father's image" (much as Walsingham sees the image of Isabella in Amelia), so she coupled with her son willingly, indeed Oedipally, with the "Fruit of that monstrous night" being Adeliza (246, V.vi. 46–75), now revealed to be the sister/daughter of Edmund himself.

Just as Walpole's *Otranto* both disguises and reflects the conflict between aristocratic and middle-class ideologies regarding inheritance, E.J. Clery has shown, his *Mysterious Mother* Gothically reenacts, half-concealing it by recalling ancient Greek incest-tragedy, the other struggle at his time "between alternative models of femininity," the "idea that desire and active sexuality are natural in a woman" in conflict with the "idea that female desire is excessive and inimical to the family" (Clery 2001: 29, 37–38), a version of the tug-of-war we have seen in the philosophy of sensibility as it infused the narrative and theatrical Gothic that Robinson continues. This entire set of conundrums therefore carries over from *The Mysterious Mother* into the violation scene in *Walsingham*, particularly if we accept, as Robinson seems to, Walpole's implication that his characters' "failings and virtues" regarding sexuality "should be treated in a way which is gender-blind" (Clery 2001: 32). Walsingham himself, like Walpole's Countess, confesses to a heinous act for which he accepts considerable responsibility, despite his excuses, and Amelia admits her own part in it to the point of neither accusing nor prosecuting him. Even though Walsingham's sin finally comes off as more forgivable than the Countess', in part because he is a man, we are left betwixt and between in our reactions as we read about his Gothic rape of Amelia behind the disguised image of Isabella. There is horror here but equally some mitigation and distancing of it basic to the Walpolean Gothic and Burkean terror, compounded this time by the legacy of Greek tragedy that leaves characters irresolvably caught, like Sophocles' Oedipus, between personal responsibility and external forces beyond their control. Are not Walsingham and Amelia, though both have failed to restrain excess feeling, as much the victims of long-standing deceptions, including counterfeit images, perpetrated by others against them as the Countess and Edmund are in *The Mysterious Mother*?

In the end, the ultimate resolutions in *Walsingham* leave its ideological quandaries just as unresolved as it leaves this question, despite seeming to do the opposite (as Gothic novels often do) with a conventional marriage in the *dénouement*. I want to defer until later most of the performance of gender-roles here, but I would argue now that the inconsistencies involved in defining the self by the image of the other expand exponentially over *Walsingham*'s final pages. The ultimate hidden secret in this novel, concealed by years of disguises and an "ivory cabinet" that holds its dead Lord's will (*WMR* 5: 129), is that Sidney, with that already gender-crossing name, has been female from the beginning, forced, before she could understand the consequences, to seem unequivocally male so that (s)he could inherit her deceased father's, now Lady Aubrey's, estate through primogeniture (5: 477). There are fitfully hopeful suggestions that this disguise can make Sidney (indeed, any cross-dresser with resources) a more fully realized human being able to be "an expert at all manly exercises" yet equally to present "a form molded by the Graces," a combination that might be taken as a picture of perfection to be emulated by, and thus to define, Walsingham and everyone (95–96). Yet this image is a paragon mainly because it is perceived to be a man's, a figure never fully linked to androgyny by anyone and hailed as more complete than any woman's. Walsingham thus sees in Sidney a rival male figure of mimetic desire, apparently wanting and attracting female love-objects desired by Walsingham himself (as on 259–264), to a point where he considers poisoning his rival until he hears that he is a she (479–480). In addition, it turns out that Sidney, once she is revealed, has nearly always found this deceptive fashioning of her appearance oppressive, keeping her from fulfilling the primary "affection of her heart" (477). That is partly because the ruse she carries out is governed by the "ancient" *Otranto*-esqe demand that the image of the primal father continue uninterrupted through primogeniture.

The chief signifier of this haunting figuration, which is no longer worthy of belief (as in Walpole's first Preface), is therefore a ghost of a counterfeit in *Walsingham*. Manifested in "Sir Sidney," it is an ongoing, if suspect, image of male continuity for every character that most immediately refers here to a will hidden away, like the "authentic writing" claimed but never produced in *Otranto* (Walpole 2003: 164). That will, once uncovered, includes bequests inscribed but never executed as written, making it evidence of out-and-out "fraud" for Walsingham (*WMR* 5: 476–477), a series of signifiers never allowed to reach their referents. This will's exposure also undoes the dominance of Lady Aubrey by exposing the deceptions she has used to achieve the illusion of power. She has always grounded her command in that document *and* its concealment, gaining sway by both asserting and usurping hidden male prerogatives. All this while, too, she has concealed her own "enslavement" to a now-dead confidante who threatened her with revelations about her family's past that could destroy its aristocratic image, the image based ultimately on the ongoing Father that she has used primogeniture to sustain by having Sidney counterfeit her sex (5: 478). Even more ironic, given all this, is the ruling "affection" of Sidney's "heart," the explanation for "Sir Sidney's" showy, if not finally sexual, attempts to seem to steer other women away from Walsingham: she has always loved only him; his, like Prince Almanza's and Lord Denmore's, has been the male image that has defined *her* the most; and it is this admission that leads Walsingham to forgive himself and her for "past sorrows" and to celebrate finally marrying her without any sense of irony (480–481). Attempts to change the definitional force of the Walpolean image of the male other (the "ancient" specter) do surface in this most complex (and, yes, "modern") of Robinson's Gothic novels, particularly when that image is rendered female and androgynous for a time. But even the new "other" himself/herself is ultimately pulled back toward the ancient stand-ard, like Theodore as clearly Alfonso's descendant at the end of *Otranto*, in this case with Sidney becoming unambiguously a woman so that Walsingham's old vision of himself as Glenowen's heir can actually be fulfilled when he marries her. In such a Janus-faced way, this Gothic fiction plays out yet another aporia between revolution and tradition deeply unresolved for both Robinson and the still-patriarchal Western culture that she knew too well. It is dubious for us, Robinson and the Walpolean Gothic suggest, to tie our self-definitions to any fixed image of an other, but, in the culture of the late eighteenth century caught between the ancient and the modern (and perhaps today?), we may not have much of a choice – or do we?

5 The Gothic Mind

Just as prominent a motif in Robinson's Gothic, particularly after her 1792 *Vancenza*, is her articulation of the human psyche as, on one level, at odds with itself and, on another, a hidden interior space described according to conflicting ideological assumptions. Her characters, usually through letters, incessantly bare their inner thoughts, deepening the mental battleground revealed via indirect discourse occasionally in Walpole's *Otranto* and more extensively in Radcliffe's romances (as in *The Mysteries of Udolpho*, e.g., in Radcliffe 1998*b*: 47–48, 125, 248, 330–331, 589–590). *Walsingham*, for instance, starts with its narrator-hero feeling himself pulled toward "dark and gloomy passions" that seem to come from an "evil demon" or "the potent hand of destiny" assumed in ancient times; it is as if these forces beyond him are causing his "errors of a too vivid imagination," though they are probably projected by him, even as they appear to generate "the miseries of sensibility" in a very eighteenth-century sense (5: 6–7). Even more than Radcliffe, Robinson imports the ancient-versus-modern interplay of the Walpolean Gothic into the individual psyche, and that oxymoronic condition is articulated by several of her characters well before it is highlighted in *Walsingham*. First, in *The Widow* three years earlier, there is Julia St. Laurence, the title figure who retires to a cottage on the grounds of Harefield Castle fearing, but not certain, that her long-lost husband is dead, like the Julia Mazzini of Radcliffe's *Sicilian Romance* who hides in a "solitary cottage" when she thinks *her* love-object has been killed (Radcliffe 1993: 105). Robinson's Julia initially describes her "state of mind" as just as retrogressive as Walsingham's, as "not susceptible of any pleasure but that which results from the recollection of scenes, past, *never to return*," memory-traces cut off from their grounds, so much that she "resign[s]" her free will to that "Being" of whose "power … we are still the creatures" (*WMR* 2: 352–353). Similarly, in Robinson's *Angelina* of 1796, with this new title character now replacing Julia as the mysterious widow-woman in a cottage attached to a "noble ruin" (*WMR* 3: 17), the principal letter-writer, Sophia of Clarendon Abbey, begins her first letter to a confidante by mentally facing "prospects" that "only fill my mind with horror and disgust"; her father is forcing her to marry a Lord Acreland for his presumed fortune, so "I cannot help meditating on the gloom of a sepulchre" (3: 6), as though death were calling her, when she contemplates entrapment in an old-style marriage. Even the title character, Count Alfrerenzi, in Robinson's *Sicilian Lover* play set mainly in the "*Gothic Hall[s]*" of sixteenth-century Italy (*WMR* 8: 68, II.v.1), exclaims that his "mind" has become "A chaos wild of gorgeous desolation," a terrifying Burkean sublimity, as he seeks his beloved Honoria withdrawn into a convent because he has avenged her by killing her tyrannical father who, Alferenzi mistakenly thinks, has killed his own daughter (8: 113, V.xv.138–145). At that point he echoes the earlier moment when Honoria fears her father's violent pursuit of the Count because he is not the husband her patriarch has chosen for her. There she feels her "ray of hope" in loving Alferenzi pulled back into "a dream of horror, where the brain" is "Stamped with the semblance of some phantom dire" (8: 69, II.v. 49–52).

The Influence of William Godwin

The paradox in all these self-revelations, given the modernity of their author at the time, is how much all these Robinson characters, while reacting to their own empirical perceptions and associations, feel subject to a force apart from their own will that seems to control their thinking as though it were an ancient preternatural power. For Robinson by the early 1790s, belief in the supernatural – never invoked, except as imagined, in her novels any more than in Radcliffe's – was still a lingering attraction to her and her readers, but usually as emptied of independent control over human destinies, as it is in the first *Otranto* Preface. It had to be replaced, then, in the ancient-versus-modern dynamic of Gothic fiction, by some other entity or process imported into thought from a more modern ideological concept, a drive that could seem externally empowered but may be more a combination of the internal and the external. Such an alternative, as Ashley Cross has shown most fully, was provided for Robinson by William Godwin, whose writings she started reading, as did other English progressives, before she met and started corresponding with him in 1796 (Cross 109). Because he too furthered the Lockean legacy of empiricism, its incorporation into the philosophy of sensibility, Robinson's own support for nonviolent revolution against the reigning class structure, and the assumptions about thought in the *Vindication* of Mary Wollstonecraft (Godwin's lover by 1796 and his wife by 1797), Robinson selectively adopted much of the theory of mind that Godwin advances in his *Enquiry Concerning Political Justice* (1793), published a year before Robinson's *The Widow*, and his Gothic novel *Things as They Are; or the Adventures of Caleb Williams* (1794), published two or more years before *Angelina, The Sicilian Lover*, and *Walsingham* (*WMR* 1: xxxvii), the last of which *Caleb Williams* influenced extensively (Cross 112–134).

The accounts of their minds divided against themselves by the central characters in these Robinson texts, after all, sound very like the confessions of Godwin's Caleb as he tells his own story. Looking back at the outset of his narrative, he proclaims both his "life" and his mind a "theatre of calamity"; his "enemy," his former employer Lord Falkland – figuratively enlarged (like Walpole's ghost of Alfonso), though actually "of small stature" (Godwin 2009: 4), by the outsized authority of his aristocratic class – haunts Caleb's thoughts quite Satanically by exhibiting a dark Radcliffean "countenance ... pregnant with meaning" (2009: 3–4), living now as a sort of fallen angel, a "mere shell" (another ghost of a counterfeit) of the Falkland who once "imbibed the love of chivalry and romance" (2009: 8–9). Because of the command over laws and the control of nearly all discourse granted to aristocrats (also magistrates) by "things as they are," Godwin is here recalling but denying once-supernatural powers over thought by transferring into thought itself, as a driving force, the mindsets promoted by a hierarchical social system, including the aristocratic striving, as in Falkland, to emulate the "ancient" forms of romance that Walpole has Gothically revived and put in question. Robinson agrees with this relocation of "demonic power" as early as *The Widow*, influenced by Godwin's *Enquiry* if not directly by *Caleb Williams*. There her manifestly Satanic seducer Lord Woodley admits to a Gothic, Hell-like psychology caused entirely by his being brought up an aristocrat: "kept in the very midnight of existence, where reason is blinded by the glories of deception, and all the purest infusions of the mind chilled into apathy" (*WMR* 2: 380). Rooting one's earthly agency ostensibly in signifiers looking vaguely back to ancient romance – however fraudulently, given the counterfeit glitter to which its signifiers have degenerated – has become a power over the mind of the self and others like, but not the same as, the transcendental forces in ancient romance itself.

Godwin's writings also draw Robinson toward Gothic visions of the mind that are filled with even more haunting inconsistencies. Near the end of his narrative, Caleb does cast himself as a supreme victim of the "injustice of society" after enduring a series of "persecutions" instigated by Falkland to ensure that a hidden past concealed by his one-time secretary can never be conveyed believably to others (Godwin 2009: 299). These harassments have followed Caleb sneaking into a Gothic "apartment" deep in Falkland's mansion and opening its secreted "iron chest" (2009: 6, 128) that recalls the "casket" in *Vancenza* and anticipates the "ivory cabinet" in *Walsingham*. This impulsive act has motivated Falkland, without he or Caleb witnessing the chest's contents at this point (indeed, the reader never sees them), to confess his killing of a rival aristocrat and his support for the hanging of two tenant farmers as guilty of that crime (2009: 128–131). Nonetheless, Caleb ultimately sees himself as just as guilty of "iniquity" as Falkland (300). He finally regards both of them as perverted by "the corrupt wilderness of society," "a 'rotten soil' of attitudes based on class hierarchies that can Gothically turn potential 'virtue' into 'deadly nightshade'" (303), not least because both Falkland and Caleb have read some of the same books (3–4). This view accords with much of the theory of mind in Godwin's *Enquiry*, where everyone's grown behavior stems from "the opinions they form" based on Lockean sense perceptions and the associations of ideas that arise from those (Godwin 1976: 107). That process for Godwin is "controlled" by the community "circumstances" in which it occurs, especially from "the education we derive from the forms of government under which we live" that can be based on a "state" of human "equality" but currently are not (113) in England's 1790s maintenance of the antiquated *in*equalities upheld by old romances (248–253). A retrograde social structure in this scheme leads to destructive individual behaviors by "necessity" because "conduct" is relentlessly driven by "the circumstances under which ... [an] intelligent being is placed" (336).

At the same time, though, Caleb in Godwin's novel, while he can indeed root Falkland's and his behavior in internalized social pressures, cannot explain his own primary error, his invasion of that private chest, by this logic, even though he too believes in an "irresistible necessity" where a motivation, once instigated, *has* to be carried into action (Godwin 2009: 134). When he retrospectively strives to account for his "fatal impulse" to penetrate one of Falkland's surfaces, as though he might gaze "on the other side of the picture" that is the Walpolean image of the defining other (2009: 113), Caleb cannot clearly describe the "infatuation" that "instantaneously seized" me (128); it is "as if my animal system had undergone a revolution" arising from "involuntary" desire (126). As Rudolf Storch has suggested, Godwin, through Caleb, is here confessing to "subterranean emotions" that were starting to become subliminal drives in pre-Freudian conceptions of the unconscious (Storch 190). Early stages of this idea were already stirring sketchily, as others have seen, in Walpole's *Otranto* (see Morris), where deep and mixed feelings arise unbidden in Manfred that are strikingly at odds with his staged persona. It is no wonder, then, that Godwin has Caleb confess in his narrative that, when he says he feels as though there is a "devil that possessed me," he means that "my mind produced a contention of opposite principles," feelings prompted by class subjugation, yes, but also a "insatiable desire of satisfaction" bursting into consciousness and driving toward "an unknown gratification" (Godwin 2009: 116, 119) – an irony emphasized by neither Caleb nor his readers beholding what is in the iron chest. "Necessity" is thus, inconsistently, an external material and public pressure detectable by everyone who will see it *and* an internal psychological force whose wellsprings and goals are unknown to anyone. Even in his *Enquiry*, Godwin has to admit that numerous "single actions," when "traced to their remotest source," can "be found to be the complex result of [many] different motives," external and internal (1976: 127).

The Widow (1794)

Developing this Godwinian-Gothic condition of the mind, Robinson renders her own version of it, pointing up its conflicts, in Gothic works that both preceded and followed *Caleb Williams*. When Julia in *The Widow* feels her thinking pulled back toward memory-traces that seem unconnectable to their past, she is actually being haunted by the rupture of those signifiers from their referents carried out most, we find, by her still-living husband – initially a second devil in this novel and then more a specter of counterfeiting – who has left her as "Sidney" and then, thinking her dead, married someone else, now as "Lord Allford," because of a gaping disconnect in his motivations (*WMR* 2: 370–371).

Writing as this "Lord," he remembers being torn from her, shortly after meeting and marrying her in Philadelphia in the 1770s (2: 370), by an internalization of Godwinian "circumstances" loaded with social prejudices: her father's "enmity" toward the English, hence his adopting the name "Sidney" (later used, we now see, as a disguise-name in *Walsingham*); his being called back to his British regiment, which would not have accepted his wedding an American, hence his concealment of it; and, once he hears, without verifying, that Julia has died in a shipwreck crossing the Atlantic, his submission to his uncle's "ambition" for him to make "an illustrious alliance" (370–371), hence his assumption of a title that his calculating second wife, now deceased, turns out to have "boasted" that she "purchased" (419). All of this makes him as much a layering of counterfeits as Lord Denmore will later be, to the point that we never know Sidney/Allford's birth-name any more than we know the contents of Falkland's iron chest. But he also resembles Caleb in confessing, yet barely expressing, a radically different motivation when he recalls his actual marriage. He cannot remember his first meeting with Julia, only "the flame which consumes the heart" and the impossibility that "time" or "change of fortune can obliterate from my heart the image of *her*" (371), much as Caleb can never get past the image of Falkland as the focus of his greatest adoration ("I love you more than I can express"; Godwin 2009: 117) as well as his hatred of tyrannical oppression, both inextricably interconnected.

This dissociation of sensibility, splitting up the roots of economics and the deepest drives toward sympathy linked together by Adam Smith from the 1750s–70s (see Poovey 1979: 307–308), seems to be healed, through it still hovers hauntingly, when Sidney/Allford and Julia finally see each other alive. He writes, in a letter of stagey exclamations, that he has joyously "clasped her faded form to my rent heart," seeing her, now ill from grief, as near death and ghost-like but not a counterfeit, and he vows to throw off any "golden chain" that might keep him from living as and where she does (*WMR* 2: 417). She, resuscitated by his return, promises to forgive him "in the poor hut of mutual affection" where they can "forget the miseries of wealthy bondage" rendered so Gothically in the rest of this novel (420). But this divorce of economics and feeling is finally short-lived, since Charles Seymour, now suddenly willing to forego his own passion for Julia, forces Lady Allford to divorce Sidney/Allford, resign her estate, and let it pass, as it does, to Sidney and Julia together (423–424). Unlike Godwin's, Robinson's readers, as in many romances, get to have it both ways: the critique of love as too tied to wealth and the tie being restored in the final pages, with aristocracy now less castigated while still remaining Gothic. Yet because this paradox is presented in a Gothic-Godwinian mode, we can see this "blend" of ancient and more modern tendencies haunting us with, while also half-veiling, our own struggle to dissociate, while we also still desire, quite different "necessities" in our minds that do not logically belong together. We may feel superficially satisfied by how this novel's resolution puts that tug-of-war at a distance, but we cannot forget the conflicted motivations staged for us in the Gothic and sentimental thinking of Sidney/Allford and the divorce of memories from their grounds, the ghosts of her husband's counterfeiting, that they cause in the mind of Julia.

Walsingham Again

Once we grasp Robinson reworking Godwin in *The Widow*, moreover, we can readily see similar dissociations between separate conceptions of the mind in her later Gothic novels. Particularly in the "violation" scene of *Walsingham*, the already self-divided hero feels pulled retrogressively toward playing out the effects of old-style primogeniture on him (the key belief driving his "circumstances") as though they were sent by a devil. He tries to possess the woman he thinks of as the love-object of the heir who has supposedly displaced him, metaphorically taking that heir's place, while also remaining immersed in a corrupt social whirl of seductive disguises that has reduced old romance to counterfeits of it. Concurrently, though, his mind is drawn just as retrogressively toward Caleb Williams' "involuntary" impulse to penetrate to the "other side of the picture." Walsingham pursues his mental portrait of Isabella behind the disguised Amelia he rapes, and he may also be anticipating the Freudian unconscious even more. He seems to be driving beyond Isabella, like Walpole's Theodore looking through *his* Isabella and seeing the dead Matilda (Walpole 2003: 165), toward dimmer memories of his long-dead mother buried on the Glenowen grounds (*WMR* 5: 20). This layering of images is reminiscent of Walpole's Narbonne Countess whom her son dimly sees, while the Countess sees the image of her husband, behind what Edmund takes to be his intercourse with an exogamous love-object in *The Mysterious Mother*. Added to the chaos of explanations behind this *Walsingham* episode, then, is a Gothic mind torn between radically different ideologies of motivation.

Angelina (1796)

In *Angelina*, too, Robinson's reworking of *The Widow* plot and its central relationship half-repeats and half-alters the conflicted motivations at the core of them. It consequently suggests another Godwinian-Gothic disconnection in the mind, this one between the force of "circumstances" and a different type of pre-Freudian preconsciousness. The title character, replacing Julia as the sequestered "widow" but without our reading any letters directly from her, is known to us, from the start, as the former and abandoned love of the fortune-hunting Lord Acreland, the same man who has accepted his role in a betrothal forced by her father onto Sophia Clarendon that could shore up the Acreland estate (*WMR* 3: 3). Not surprisingly, he has drifted away from the young Angelina he married in secret and left there (3: 308–309) because, like Lord Woodley in *The Widow*, he has been so "pleased with the variety of luxuries that assailed my passions" in the aristocratic world that after years away in "the obliterating intercourse" of "society" – his Godwinian "circumstances" – he has too easily come to believe in several counterfeit rumors: first, in Angelina being naïve enough to credit a "report" of his "fall[ing] in a duel in Italy" (132); second, in gossip about her "finding consolation" with his "domestic chaplain" back home (132); and third, in the lie from the conniving Lady Selina, his sister, that Angelina has "died in Wales" (135). Now, however, that a living Angelina has been sighted by a friend in a secluded ruin, Acreland shifts his style of discourse abruptly, scribbling that "I am wild with reflection! . . . I feel my own unworthiness; I shrink at the idea of her superiority!" (131). Shocked into resurrecting a long-repressed memory of a "bosom, where all the virtues, all the graces live with transcendent lustre" and distancing this fixed and sanctified image from all that has been said about her since, Acreland laments that Angelina is now "the melancholy inmate of a spot so dreary" and that he must live with "the miseries of self-reproach" (131).

This thought-process, set so apart from his immediate circumstances, anticipates the nature of melancholy as Freud defines it in "Mourning and Melancholia" (1917). There melancholia is focused on the image of a "loss," which can be the death but need not be, "of a loved person . . . or some abstraction that has taken the place of one" (Freud 1953–1974: 14: 243). This image, with melancholics, becomes an "object-loss" that can be "withdrawn from consciousness" for long periods of time, like Acreland's years away from the Angelina he married (Freud 14: 245). By so deeply holding on to this lost object, the melancholic "turn[s] . . . away from reality" and "cling[s]" to it "through the medium of a hallucinatory wishful psychosis" and, when he becomes suddenly half-conscious of it, "he reproaches himself" and "expects to be cast out and punished" just as Acreland shows in his self-accusing exclamations (14: 244–246). The result, as we see in *Angelina*, is a preconscious "*identification* of the ego with the abandoned object," so much so that "the ego wants to incorporate the object into itself" to a point where, often as an abstraction, it disappears from consciousness for long stretches, even as it also prevents desire being "displaced on another object" (14: 249), hence Acreland's inability to love Sophia as more than an "expedient" (*WMR* 3: 3). At the root of this process, after all, is "narcissistic identification" (14: 253), the other seen as the defining image of the self so basic for Robinson to Gothic/ sentimental desire and now, we see, to the Gothic mind. Godwin, by splitting up the "necessities" in the mind, has inspired in *Angelina* yet another bifurcation, reminiscent of Caleb Williams holding on to his original "loved" image of Falkland as one "of a noble nature" at the end of his narrative, where his thoughts push aside all of his master's predations to keep this "figure . . . ever in imagination before me" as a defining other still (Godwin 2009: 300).

Angelina, meanwhile, also presents us with another divided state of mind that is quite literally "Gothic," given that term's eighteenth-century drift between meanings. When we read Sophia's first letter, we see that she was once "fond of Clarendon Abbey" in all its Gothic antiquity but that now, forced into a prospective marriage to an older man apparently to maintain its grandeur, she, like Walpole's Isabella, regards every such structure as a gigantic "sepulchre" imposing past oppressions and hierarchies onto her present life (*WMR* 3: 6). Later, too, when she finds shelter from her father's dictates at South Cliff Castle, she starts out, after hearing legends about "haunted" spaces there (3: 210), by holding "all stories of supernatural appearances in utmost contempt" (3: 219), becoming momentarily even more modern than a Radcliffe heroine. Still, she feels the terror of just such characters when she explores South Cliff's dark chapel, hears sounds she cannot explain, and feels "something glid[ing]" by her in the obscurity (221), the Burkean terror sublime in full cry. It seems to her mind as if "the events of past ages, the sufferings of the innocent, and the tyranny of rulers" enveloped by shadows can suddenly reemerge from the dark, "awaken[ing] a thousand reflections" on their horrors despite their absence (213). Even so, Sophia writes elsewhere, "my heart pants for the solitudes of Clarendon Abbey . . . the wilderness, the grotto, the hermitage . . . All my favorite retreats" of Edenic "consolation" (20) connected to her place of birth, here more maternal than patriarchal. Sophia's mind oscillates between the ideological conceptions of the "dark" and the "white Gothic," which, as we noted earlier, contended with each other from the early 1700s right through the 1790s.

Angelina, who (again) never writes for herself, is made to play out much the same dichotomy by her observers in the "old castle" ruin to which she retires. On the one hand, she is thought of as "the poor mad lady" who is semi-imprisoned in a dark tower because of her irrational longings for a troubled past (*WMR* 3: 17); on the other, for those same observers she is the inhabitant styled like Mother Nature, the *genius loci* of a picturesque, dimly antiquated "scene," that could have been painted (as are so many Radcliffe descriptions) by "the fancy of a Claude Lorraine" and "the pencil of a Salvator Rosa" (3: 70), both seventeenth-century landscape artists who crafted an idealized antiquity by combining layers of mythology and art history (3: 350 n.94–95). By the time the novel concludes, Angelina is even revealed as the biological mother of Sophia's true love, "Charles" but really "Frederick" (3: 340–341), and so can be remembered by the reader as the original maternal presence in, and emerging from, an idealized, if also ruined, dark-*and*-white medieval past. At one point in this novel, it seems as if an androgynous "freedom [that] lives in the mind" of us all can imaginatively sweep away the dark Gothic and install the white one in the vacated space (3: 213), replacing the ongoing spectral Father (Walpole's Alfonso) with the primal, sympathetic Mother as the benignly haunting site of human origins, the Angel-ina kept at a desired primal point beyond all the words of the letters about her. Nevertheless, all the women in this novel are caught between the Gothic drive that can still pull thought backward toward frightening retrogressions and the Gothic counter that can offer our minds a more modern, more feminine alternative, albeit one still seen through the eyes of older male artists (including Walpole and Godwin) who are caught themselves between regressive and progressive thinking in *their* Gothic minds.

Meanwhile, in addition, the Robinsonian-Gothic mind is, in the words of Godwin's Caleb, a *"theater* of calamity." Expanding on the penchant for theatricality in the Walpolean Gothic and her own career as a performer both on stage and in the fashionable world, Robinson sees the mind as invaded and occupied by the social realm of role-playing, declamation, and reaction/counter-reaction that *is* the Godwinian "community" determining patterns of thought. Consequently, her Gothic characters, even while writing letters, often feel themselves in theatrical roles when they look inward. Yet, as they do, they find themselves compelled to articulate deep, nontheatrical mental drives, which the theater of social interaction can help them haltingly express but which its stagecraft can neither control nor explain. This tension is quite apparent in *Walsingham*, especially in the blatant theatricality that envelops the whole "violation" sequence, but it turns out to be just as insistent in Robinson's other Gothic works of the mid-1790s. Julia in *The Widow*, for a time, thinks herself "fortunate" for having adopted "a *feigned name*" and "preserved the mystery of my birth" with the opaque surface she presents in her costume of "widow's weeds" (*WMR* 2: 391). But this self-staging for her is designed to protect, by concealing within her thoughts, "*his* whose name is engraved on my heart," the "form" of her likely dead husband that is her hidden mental center (2: 391–392). While this phrasing does echo Shakespeare's Hamlet keeping the words of this father's Ghost "Within the book and volume of my brain" (*Hamlet* I.v.103; Shakespeare 1974: 1150), it also takes that speech's transfer from the stage to the internalized page and transfigures it into what we have already found in Robinson's Gothic: a ghostly Lockean first impression that has been so reinforced by associations that it has become the deeply retained figure of Julia's defining second self, the "abstraction" of a love-object apparently lost into a melancholic's ingested image that no stagecraft can touch. When this Julia-figure becomes Angelina seen only from outside herself in the novel named for her, too, the George Fairford who observes her in her Gothicized retreat has to stage her and her setting while writing about her from memory as a "countenance ... pictured on my brain" with a "roaring ... cataract" gushing behind her near the ruin where she resides (*WMR* 3: 64). In doing so, he unfolds a whole stage-scene, while also alluding to Leonardo's *Mona Lisa*, that he and the reader observe as if they are members of an audience. Indeed, Angelina in her novel is nearly always dramatized for us so as to display the theatrically inflected mindset of her different observers. This time, though, George adds his memory of Angelina floating across the scene by recalling "the phantom which vanished when I pursued it" (3: 64) as a spectral and mobile part of his scene-painting, a scheme of artistic construction he licenses even further by comparing his thought-pattern to Claude and Salvator (3: 70). But such landscapes or stagings cannot capture such a specter-in-motion, and so George really cannot either. Here Angelina's image as he remembers it is more like the ghostly, shifting impressions that Terry Castle has seen in the novels of Radcliffe, where characters believe they have seen a figure in a landscape that is really their fleeting spectral memory of a once-perceived countenance mentally projected into the setting (as in Radcliffe 1998*b*: 114–115), an image perceived but never substantially "there" that escapes theatricalization.

The Sicilian Lover (1796)

Robinson extends this self-division, while complicating it in yet another way, when she writes for the theater itself in *The Sicilian Lover*. Godwin's influence reappears in this play when Honoria struggles to explain her "mingling labyrinths of thought" (*WMR* 8: 62; I.iii.238), torn as she is between her own passion, here for Count Alferenzi, and her love for her father, the Marquis Valmont, who has dictatorially betrothed her to young Prince Montalva. On the one hand, though she firmly asserts "my freedom" to choose her spouse (8: 55; I. i.79), she is so braised by her upbringing (her Godwinian circumstances) to maintain "my noble name" (8: 56; I.i.93) that her attraction to Alferenzi is substantially based on his being of "loftiest birth," Sicilian or not (8: 61; I. iii.212). On the other hand, due to her forced isolation under her father's misogynistic control, Honoria readily believes the "rumours," later proven false, that her "father" himself may have caused her deceased mother's "death" (I.iii.253–254). It is this association in her thoughts of Valmont's "fierce tempest" directed against Alferenzi (I.iii.268) and the dark image of her father as her mother's secret killer that makes her feel as if her "brain" is "Stamped with the semblance of some phantom dire" (8: 69; II.v.51–52), a figure which only she sees in her "mind's eye," to quote *Hamlet* (I.ii.186; Shakespeare 1145), while she also echoes the Prince of Demark impressing his father's Ghost on his "brain." Honoria has taken impressions already ghost-like and reinforced them with anticipatory associations to produce a Shakespearean and Radcliffian spectralization almost entirely mental. It does prefigure a death in the night (8: 72; II.v.109–122) – Valmont stabbing young Montalva thinking him to be Alferenzi, reworking *The Mysterious Mother'*s mistaken identity in the dark – but that is not the anticipation to which Honoria's "phantom" refers when she thinks of it. At the same time, it also grounds itself in a false rumor about her father. It is the ghost of at least two disappointments, then, that never gets materialized outside her own thoughts in the ways Honoria sees it, so it hovers between reacting to what has been staged and haunting her with its separate existence in her thoughts alone.

Later, this indecision in the characters and the audience is redoubled when Alferenzi beholds a "blood-stain'd scarf" (8: 81; II.ix.364) that makes him think Honoria has been murdered by her father (II.ix.366) only to have that view refuted right after he stabs Valmont, who himself thinks Alferenzi a "Horrible spectre" of the man he thinks he has killed in the dark (8: 91; III.ix.211). Just then Alferenzi sees Honoria herself emerge alive from a grotto, whereupon he calls *her* a "spirit" at first (8: 93; III.ix.237), before realizing that several "dread coincidence[s] of time and act" (III.ix.278) have exposed a series of yawning differences between what minds have imagined and what onstage appearances have revealed. It is hardly surprising that Alferenzi describes his "mind" as a Burkean cacophony "of gorgeous desolation" in the end, since he also finds that "the pressure heap'd upon the brain" from this onslaught of staged images "o'erwhelms the active faculties of thought," which can nevertheless claim some independence from them, if only enough to misinterpret them and go its own way (8: 113; V.xv.142–145). There has always been that problem we noted earlier with the theatricality in Walpole's and then Godwin's Gothic. It is hard to tell how much the mind is formed most: by outside forces and reactions to actions like those on a stage or by internal modifications of impressions via associations of ideas or preconscious impulses. For Robinson this conflict becomes *the* central conundrum in *The Sicilian Lover*. The mind here cannot tell where the "pressures" of the stagelike world on it and where the mind's supposed "freedom" from outside pressures (Honoria's initial claim) begin and end, even though there continues to be an assumed distinction between the two and a desire, even hope, for the liberty of thought to overcome its circumstances.

For Robinson the Gothic mind – imaged often like a Janus-faced tug-of-war between the ancient and the modern, as we have now seen – is finally a layering of oscillations between external and internal causes of thought where each blurs into the other even as they try to become separate. As though he were summing all this up, she has her Walsingham put it this way: "the mind of man is a chaos of perpetual warfare; the affections of our early days," which are soon transfigured into role-plays on the stage of the social world, ultimately "combat with the propensities of nature," the more primal drives, so much so that the mind always has to "struggle in the fetters of contradiction" (*WMR* 5: 46). Gothic writing from Walpole to Robinson, if true to itself, cannot depict the human psyche in any other way.

6 The Gothic Performance of Gender

Gothic and its theatricality, it also turns out, are just as conflicted when they articulate the presentation of gender, that coalescence of cultural signifiers supposedly anchored to biological sex that, as *Walsingham* has shown us, can float away from that grounding across multiple locations, even in the self-fashioning of single individuals. Such is the case in the inaugural "Gothic Story," where all the *Otranto* "actors" stick predominantly to already-staged types, each with its established inconsistencies: Manfred as the male "savage tyrant" despite internal misgivings (Walpole 2003: 87); Theodore with his princely "gallantry" shining through his peasant guise (2003: 108); and Matilda, Isabella, and even Hippolita with their Richardsonian female attitudes of "disinterested [meaning 'unselfish'-] warmth" toward each other and usually toward men (101) as they try, like Pamela and Clarissa, to both resist excessive male predations and avoid any postures of excessive female dominance. These stances are so insistently maintained that they can readily be paralleled to others like them, with Manfred resembling the portrait of his guilt-ridden grandfather, Theodore the picture of Alfonso unarmored, and Matilda and Isabella so alike that they are mistaken for each other more than once. Such an overinsistence on by-now-ancient standards, then, inherently puts the solidity of sex roles in question, opening them, at least somewhat, to more modern understandings of their tired conventionality and their transferability, especially when Manfred's public posture is declared disconnected from his inner conflicts. True, when these characters try stepping out of these roles, as when Manfred (87) and Theodore (165) doubt their public positions or when both Matilda and Isabella openly defy Manfred to enable Theodore's escape (108, 128), they place themselves in danger of subterranean darkness, violent death, and/or confusion over love-objects

(165) and even sexual orientation, as when Manfred, supposedly chasing Isabella, "flushed by wine and love . . . come[s] to seek" her father, Frederic, for a whole "night" of "revelling" (158). Yet the juxtaposition of these terrifying openings onto murky, unknown levels alongside mostly conventional patterns of being is precisely what puts the readers and characters of Walpolean Gothic in its *differend* state of tension between lingering antiquated and rising progressive schemes of understanding.

This state clearly encompasses gender-crossing as much as gender instability when the Walpolean Gothic is intensified by Matthew Lewis's *The Monk* of early 1796, likely an influence as much as Godwin on Robinson's later novels (see, for example, *WMR* 4: 85–89). Ambrosio, *The Monk*'s title character, is tempted into unpriestly and pansexual abandon when he finds himself "attracted" to the boy-novice "Rosario" (Lewis 67) only to find "him" to be a cover-figure for the succubus-"enchantress" "Matilda" (a Walpolean name radically transfigured; Lewis 79–85). "She" then prompts him to unleash his unbounded sexuality to the point of drawing him toward both her voluptuous femininity and a "manliness" in her manner (210) and down to a subterranean meeting with a "beautiful . . . youth" who turns out to be "Lucifer" himself (243–244), the ultimate ambisexual tempter – and backstage director of Ambrosio's theatrical world – who has always controlled Matilda, originally a shape-shifting spirit with no inherent sex (361). By the time of Robinson's later Walpolean writing, the Gothic performance of gender, which first shows itself as a transferable signifier of older signifiers, has become a spectral play of counterfeits referring to counterfeits where definite gender boundaries and sexual orientations threaten to dissolve, even as they keep insisting on redeclaring themselves. Robinson, of course, was especially well positioned in her own succession of roles on and off stage to take performative gender fluidity back through the Gothic to its roots in Shakespeare. In the late 1770s, as Viola in *Twelfth Night* and Rosalind in *As You Like It* (*WMR* 1: xxxv), she played his women disguised as young men (the cross-dressing that the Prince asked her to repeat outside the theater), characters who reveal when each play ends that they have always been women yet who were in fact all played by young men in the theater of Shakespeare's time.

Walsingham Once More

Consequently, spurred probably, but not only, by *The Monk,* the performance of gender takes center stage increasingly in Robinson's Gothic novels from late 1796 to 1799, alongside resistances to its revolutionary implications. *Walsingham* provides the most flagrant example, as evidence from it has already

shown. True, "Sir Sidney" is not only a Gothic figure. S/he was surely influenced by a publicized phenomenon that Robinson notes in her *Letter to the
Women of England* (*WMR* 8: 152–153): the Chevalier D'Eon, an apparently
male ambassador from France "who in 1777 declared that he was a woman"
and, once s/he was dismissed as an ambassador, "made an income in public
fencing" (Shaffer 2002: 77–78), a sport Sir Sidney does take up (*WMR* 5: 96).
Yet it is only after *The Monk* that Robinson offers such a figure in a Gothic
novel; like Matilda there, Sir Sidney here is an initially obscure being first
presented to the title character in a seductive male guise through the machin-
ations of a secret plotter: Lady Aubrey under the influence of her confidante, the
Satanic Mrs. Blagden, who has long sought revenge on Walsingham, the son of
the man who has seduced and betrayed her (*WMR* 5: 478–479). This layering of
a Gothic figuration over a public celebrity produces a multi-leveled character
rich with implications, and recent scholarship has rightly brought these out. As
Eleanor Ty has written, *Walsingham* prefigures "what Judith Butler calls the
'performativity of gender'" (Ty 43) enacted by what we see in Sir Sidney: "a
regularized and constrained repetition of norms" coded as male but performable
in mixtures with ones coded female (Ty 46, using Butler's words). There thus
comes to be such a blurring of boundaries in this Gothic transvestite, as in
Lewis' Matilda, that s/he "unsettles [all] conventional thinking about sexual
differences and, perhaps, even sexual preferences" (Ty 49). S/he has the freedom to play out many behaviors usually restricted to men, all while retaining
"the spontaneous effusions of the heart" most associated with women yet also
apparent in Mackenzie's *Man of Feeling* (*WMR* 5: 95–96). In addition, as Julie
Shaffer has emphasized, "Sidney's cross-dressing ... leads to the novel's play
with male homosexual desire" (Shaffer 2002: 72). Walsingham's confessed
attraction to the "handsome" physical beauty of this more complete person
(*WMR* 5: 95) Gothically echoes Manfred's seeking of Frederic when "flushed"
by "wine and love," Caleb Williams' "love" for Lord Falkland, and Ambrosio's
sensual attraction toward the "boy" Rosario. At "the same time" that
Walsingham is "questioning the limits placed on the female sex," then, it is
also "reconfiguring masculine character" through its hero, making him act
through and ruminate over "scenes of sympathy and suffering" normally
enacted by women in sentimental fiction (Ty 51–52) well beyond – for example,
in the "violation" sequence – what we see in the men of Mackenzie or Godwin.

Nonetheless, *Walsingham* draws back from fully embracing these very implications while it continues to castigate "the arbitrary nature of the way [Western]
culture distributes class [and gender] privileges," too often to "those who wear
the right clothes" (Ty 55). In the end, even more emphatically than Viola and
Rosalind, Sidney must be revealed as unequivocally feminine, just as

steadfastly as she has always loved Walsingham heterosexually, the reason she actively tempts women away from him and so flirts with lesbianism while remaining his woman. As Walsingham finally writes, "every affection of her heart is beautifully feminine," making her "masculine habits" admirable augmentations up to a point, but characteristics ultimately governed by the center of her being that has never fundamentally changed (*WMR* 5: 478). For him her essence even exists at this point above and beyond the Lockean and Godwinian development of his mind. "The prejudices" inculcated into him from "early infancy," Walsingham concludes, "are completely counteracted by the ... heroic virtues of my transcendent Sidney," as though she reincarnates the perfectly feminine "Una" – echoing even the "hidden care" this "lovely Ladie" carries (Spenser 7, I.i.4) – in Book I of Edmund Spenser's *The Faerie Queene* (1595), a late-stage epitome of "ancient romance."

This conclusion, it has to be said, is both enabled and put in question by sporadic attacks within the novel on what *Walsingham* often celebrates: gendered performativity and expansions of what womanhood can encompass. The possibility in Gothic performance of divorcing signifiers from reliable referents and enacted behavior from a self-determined inner life, as in Walsingham echoing Caleb Williams and Sidney echoing Walpole's Manfred, is satirically excoriated when this novel introduces "polygraphs." These are followers of the hero's most playful aristocratic friend who "ape [his] dress and manners as close as one's own shadow" and become his constant "phantoms" reenacting what he does and wears, suggesting that the "proud originality" of "our ancestors" has been turned into the "caprices" of "the present generation" (*WMR* 5: 353–354) – a satire that redounds on the current aristocrats being imitated too, as well as on the Gothic's emptying-out of the very figures it imitates from ancient romance to make itself "Gothic." Perhaps because this type of other types, as Brewer tells us, was borrowed from a 1795 comedy by Hannah Cowley (*WMR* 5: xx), Robinson's insertion of it critiques both the kind of novel that *Walsingham* is and the performativity of its Sir Sidney, who seems a model of inclusive masculinity mainly by aping the most established surface behaviors of fashionable males. All that finally appears to separate him/her from a polygraph is her supposedly authentic, consistent, and "transcendent" femininity behind and beyond her disguise.

To keep that core womanhood from encompassing too much, though, as it threatens to in the wide range of Sidney's behaviors, *Walsingham* contrasts this paragon in her final form with other female characters who stage their femininity by betraying what s/he seems to render as Woman's best combination of qualities. Lady Aubrey and Mrs. Blagden, for example, embrace the decadent masculinity of "trying to control the circulation of wealth" themselves through a backstage management of the very primogeniture that most ensures male dominance, while even sympathetic women such as Amelia, who ask for seduction by fixating on one male image rather than trying to be more self-defining, can never escape men "projecting" their "libidinousness" on them (and thus blaming the victim) just as Walsingham does with both Isabella and Amelia (Shaffer 2002: 75–76). All such characters project referents into specters of counterfeits that are really ghosts of counterfeits themselves which try to look back to something transcendent that should, like primogeniture, now be seen as empty of lasting meaning. At the same time, Sidney participates in, and often encourages, all of this for eighteen years in Robinson's novel. Consequently, as seemingly transcendent in the end while supposedly having been so all along in her counterfeit act, especially since some "male" characteristics she performs ought to be parts of a greater womanhood in the future, s/he cannot escape, any more than Walsingham, from being a Gothic figuration. S/he and *Walsingham* the novel revive an ancient gendered essence by way of a haunting modern counterfeit that tries to refill the old standard with new elements while playing that quest out in a theatrical/narrative/epistolary/satiric/tragicomic performance that is as torn between conflicting attitudes as it is between modes of discourse.

Hubert de Sevrac (1796)

Such wrestlings with the performance of gender, not surprisingly, pervade other late Robinson novels as well, and two of these rework the conflicts in this Gothic motif to make distinctive suggestions of their own. Of these two, *Hubert de Sevrac* in late 1796 seems apparently less concerned with gender distinctions than with uniting the different sexes and generations in furthering the aims of the French Revolution from 1789–91 while condemning the violence of the Reign of Terror from 1792–4, which Robinson lamented in 1793 poems about the execution of Marie Antionette, whom her *Memoirs* recall her meeting in 1781 (*WMR* 1: xxxv, xxxvii, 193–194, 240–251; 7: 269). Though influenced by Charlotte Smith's *Desmond* (1792), *The Emigrants* (1793), and *The Banished Man* (1794), all sympathetic to the Revolution but alarmed by its effects (*WMR* 1: xxiii;), however, *Hubert* was "written in direct imitation of Radcliffe's ... Mysteries of Udolpho*" (Close 176), noted by its reviewers at the time (Brewer 2006: 116) and widely regarded by 1795 as Walpolean Gothic at its best. As *Udolpho* does with its heroine, Emily St. Aubert, Robinson's novel has its main characters – the French aristocrat "Hubert," his British wife (also an "Emily"), and his daughter, "Sabina" – forced to leave their original home and journey across many locales in France and Italy, to the point of being diverted by a storm at sea (*WMR* 4: 257), being terrified of relics secreted in, or moans emanating from, dark interior spaces (4: 15–16, 87–88, 228–232, 261–264), and eventually finding physical explanations for the seemingly supernatural (4: 267–272). But *Hubert* departs emphatically from *Udolpho*, set in the 1580s with its vague "turbulence" in Paris kept far from its characters and events (Radcliffe 1998*b*: 11), by making the Revolution an immediate reality, as well as the primary haunting specter, from which Robinson's characters are in flight in 1792 and which threatens to overtake them. As a result, the Gothic performance of gender in *Udolpho* is both echoed at times and pointedly revised by Walpolean means in *Hubert*, where – in a novel that dared to challenge the conservative "political reaction in England" of the 1790s (Brewer 2006: 119) – this very enactment in female and male figures, by their playing out major character changes, connects them in the end with true revolutionary progress, even as it remains linked to ancient throwbacks impossible to jettison entirely.

Some gender-specific transformations have occurred in *Hubert* before the main action begins. Recalling the transferability of "Gothic" as a term, Robinson shifts the name "Emily" to Hubert's wife and Sabina's mother, providing Sabina with a living exemplar unlike the dead mother in *Udolpho* and continuing her author's penchant for maternal legacies passed down to daughters. As Anne Close has shown, *Hubert*'s Emily brings to the novel a history of ever-changing female performances, from "marrying against her family's will" and being disinherited to "endur[ing] her husband's attachments to other women," joining him with the lower classes in prison (like Robinson), and becoming sexually experienced herself, all of which Radcliffe's Emily is "pressured" by but never lives through prior to *Udolpho*'s conclusion (Close 178). It is this range of enacted experience that enables Robinson's Emily to "guide" her daughter through "the maze of traumas" that several men try to "inflict" on her by assuming the long-standing entitlements of patriarchs (Close 178–179). One result is that Sabina begins the novel as a Walpolean actor already sympathetic to dispossession and openly critical of too much patriarchal privilege. Somewhat as *Otranto*'s Matilda frees the "peasant" Theodore by disobeying the orders of her father the "prince" (Walpole 2003: 108), Sabina challenges her father over his cavalier attitudes toward a tenant "villager" by asking "is it not barbarous . . . to drive [such a] being to despair, who has not acquired the means of guarding against its approach?" (*WMR* 4: 5). Even her aristocratic standing is put in question by her own speeches, so she gradually starts acting increasingly outside it, more than, say, Robinson's Honoria does in *The Sicilian Lover*.

Nevertheless, Madamoiselle de Sevrac must first make major changes in her feminine performance, extending the potential in Walpole's Matilda, to accord with the Revolution's best objectives. At this initial point, as Orianne Smith observes, her "interest in the plight of the peasant" is tied to "pastoral fiction," which she plays out, like her aristocratic class and father, according to "narratives of romance" (*WMR* 4: xix–xx). That derivative character-stage needs to be emptied out and refilled with empirical observations of the truly dispossessed. Moreover, like Radcliffe heroines and most young women in Lewis' *Monk*, Sabina starts out performatively in thrall to the deceptive Catholic belief-system that has long sustained the *ancien régime*. From her "earliest days," the "poison" of that kind of "superstition" (one of her Godwinian circumstances) has taken "root" in "her mind"; hence she drives herself early on to make confession in an antiquated "chapel" where "a gothic door" opens onto an inner sanctum, which itself harbors the "athletic form and countenance" (like Ambrosio's in *The Monk*; Lewis 47) of the conniving Abbot "Palerma" showing "no traits of abstinence or humiliation" (*WMR* 4: 85–86). This disappointment in what Gothic signifiers have led her to expect has, at first, no psychological effect on Sabina, since its setting as she sees it, as with the early, naive Emily in *Udolpho* (Radcliffe 1998*b*: 68), leaves her still "believing herself . . . under . . . [the] observation of some supernatural power" (4: 87). Still, Sabina does act her way out of this feminine posture by dramatically confronting the emptiness behind the old Catholic sign-system, which she finally sees as Gothic theater in which she has played the part of a female believer more devout than Radcliffe's Emily. Confronted with Palerma as a counterfeit on several levels paid to lure her into marrying the son of the rival for her father's estate (shades, again, of *Otranto*), she sees that the "hypocrisy that insults religion," as in The *Monk* and the first *Otranto* Preface, "glare[s] through the mask of sanctity worn by the Abbot," making her realize that she has always been playing the obedient Catholic female to an "approving multitude" that has valued and included that mask (*WMR* 4: 134). For a time, this "extreme of credulity" is "succeeded" in Sabina's stance by the "most obstinate skepticism" (134), another confining script where all signifiers are equally empty of truth. But it is already clear that "reason and experience" gleaned in scenes to come will soon allow her "heart" to "dilate with justice" more expansively (135). "She will become a Godwinian rather than a Radcliffe heroine" (Brewer 2006: 132), again a role but a better one, devoted to Godwin's script of reform in *Political Justice*. She will even acquire enough independence from patriarchal and priestly dominance to stand up, more than Walpole's Matilda, to the conflicted and deceptive physiognomy (briefly like *The Italian's* Schedoni) of her would-be lover, Edmund St. Clair, with a "strength of returning fortitude" beyond mere jealousy when he calls her by the name of another woman (*WMR* 4: 202).

The gendered role-transitions of the men in *Hubert* also follow this general arc toward a revolution that eventually leaves old-style violence behind, but the stagey transformation in one of them is unexpectedly tortuous compared to the more straightforward development of the title character. The Marquis de Sevrac, fleeing from the Revolution's targeting of his class with both a Mackenzian "feeling heart" and "dignified sense of [male] honor" given the "menace of disgrace" (4: 3) – a Janus-faced stance recalling Godwin's Falkland as well as Walpole's Manfred – at first keeps trying, as Orianne Smith says, to "abide by a chivalric code of honour" for men, an emptied-out script that "no longer applies" in the "world of the eighteenth century" (*WMR* 4: x). Though he subsequently attempts theatrically "rescu[ing] a series of damsels in distress" based too often on misunderstandings (x), all the disconnects (including these) that he sees between appearance and reality, reminiscent of the many counterfeits in his aristocratic life, lead him to realize that a better script has been "obscured by the intervening glooms of tyranny and oppression" (4: 266). The greater alternative, in Smith's apt words, is Hubert acting out a "reformation of patriarchal authority in personal and public life" that can ultimately dissipate the patriarchy of the *ancien régime* as well (4: xi). St. Clair, in turn, also embraces this vision (and Sabina) in the end, but by a more regressive route. This character replays the role of "Valancourt," the love-interest of the heroine in *Udolpho*. That gallant is diverted from his devotion to Radcliffe's Emily by the "snares" of Paris, including a "captivating Marchioness" and gambling that plunges him into "confinement" for "debt" (Radcliffe 1998*b*: 652), so much so that he must abjectly repent at Emily's feet, verbally enacting what he calls a "second death" while refuting exaggerated "slanders" about him in order to be born again through a virgin's forgiveness (1998b: 668). But St. Clair turns out to have been much worse. While hesitantly playing court to Sabina, he has been secretly, albeit unhappily, married all along to please his father, though he has been estranged from his wife, who really, like the second Lady Acreland in *Angelina*, sought only the "phantom" of his title (WMR 4: 258). He has then compounded that duplicity by taking up with opera dancer "Rosine D'Orvelle" – the name he mistakenly addresses to Sabina when he first sees her again (4: 202), recalling the *Otranto* mistaking of one woman for another – having been so "blinded by the brilliancy of" this "conquest" that he confesses to having "purchase[d Rosina's] favors" (4: 214–215). Thus playing a specter of counterfeiting over and over, while also seeing women as objects of exchange, like other Robinson men, St. Clair echoes Valancourt's "second death" in words by coming close to shooting himself physically before Sabina; in one of this novel's most stagey moments, she immediately cries out that his death would mean her "annihilation" too, whereupon their complete agreement on this point elevates their performances almost operatically, and St. Clair can recast their interchange as a "geniality of souls" that "can love without debasement" from now on (4: 258). At such moments, it is as if sheer Gothic performance, actors of different genders asserting the same *Liebestod* on the stage set of an old Neopolitan villa, can in fact overcome the long-standing enactment of those differences and can recast well-established characters into a transcendent, but still theatrical, dimension, one that could also model a nonviolent liberation out of and beyond the Revolution.

In the full text of *Hubert de Sevrac*, however, Robinson and the Gothic cannot let character or society change because of performance alone, even though this novel's climaxes anticipate Robinson's *Memoirs* staging her life as an ascent across roles. After all, she uses the Gothic scene of her nativity there to establish an elevated mindset of "mournful meditation" as her birthright, a constant to which she will return repeatedly. Sabina's initial sympathy for the dispossessed in *Hubert*, then, given her mother's history, is really an immutable trait of fellow-feeling that she has inherited from the female line and will surface more and more, muted only temporarily here by her being "superstitiously credulous in points of religion" (*WMR* 4: 168), an "ancient" text increasingly regarded as empty and replaced with a pro-Revolutionary state of mind that now seems generations old. On his side, Hubert's multi-leveled physiognomy, even when he is reduced to "poverty," still "display[s]" the "graces" of his "polished" Godwinian education but also a more fundamental essence that is undeniably "*manly* and prepossessing" (*WMR* 4: 166, my italics). He consequently convinces one of his would-be judges that he has been falsely accused of a murder just because "the majesty of truth beamed in de Sevrac's eyes"; here his Gothic physiognomy is not ambiguous but "the index of a soul, brave and exalted," which is fundamentally masculine (4: 178). Even St. Clair as written, whom Robinson so obviously wants to move from the libertine-male role to a gender-neutral sensibility equal to Sabina's, shows this latter mentality to be already in him even before his repentance. He repeatedly utters his natural inclination "to contemplate objects which infuse the most pleasing melancholy" just like Radcliffe's heroines (4: 248), the very scheme of thought that Robinson's *Memoirs* want to claim as her essential mindset from birth through death. This strain throughout *Hubert*, when set beside its foregroundings of performance, recalls the contrast in Walpole's *Otranto* between Manfred the internally conflicted role-player and the "steady" Theodore, inherently "noble, handsome, and commanding," a proto-King Arthur however he is dressed because he has inherited the essence of Alfonso (Walpole 2003: 108). *Hubert de Sevrac* is genuinely determined to hollow out ancient romance and old Catholicism in its performances of gender, suggesting that this tactic is profoundly necessary for nonviolent Revolution. Yet, like Walpole's whole Gothic mode, it cannot finally resist some lingering belief in the God-given essence within a personality that ancient romance was often designed to affirm.

The Natural Daughter (1799)

To be sure, it could be argued that Robinson's fiction finally does escape from this paradox in *The Natural Daughter*, her last novel, perhaps because it scales down her use of Walpolean Gothic. Her semi-autobiographical heroine in this case, the "Martha Bradford" who becomes "Mrs. Morley," consents to a marriage with an apparently "pleasing" variation on Thomas Robinson (*WMR* 7: 26). She confronts just how much of a traditional patriarch Mr. Morley is when, impelled by "her benignant propensities" while wandering his estate, she decides to take in the infant "Frances," born out of wedlock to a desperately impoverished woman she meets (7: 29–34), the not-especially Gothic "natural daughter" of the title (Robinson 2003: 28–29). She shows such devotion to little "Fanny" that her husband exiles her from his house, thinking the baby Martha's, whom he curses as an adulteress (7: 46–52), rather than acknowledging what Fanny turns out to be: an illegitimate daughter of *his* long concealed and forgotten behind his Falkland-like façade of upper-class male propriety (7: 186–188). As Sharon Setzer has established, this choice reflects Robinson's "sympathetic identification with women like Mary Wollstonecraft, the mother of another illegitimate Frances conceived in revolutionary France" (Robinson 2003: 28). Martha's break from her husband, moreover, inspired by Robinson's own life *and* her admiration for Wollstonecraft, launches this novel's heroine into performing one un-lady-like role after another: from reviving her "masculine hoyden" frankness with her parents (*WMR* 7: 4) to becoming an actress quickly cast in leading parts (83–84), a writer of novels (109), a teacher of girls (115–116), an anti-aristocratic poet (126–136), and ultimately the savior of her cast-off mother (142–144) – making *Martha* a "natural daughter" in the morality of sensibility – all in contrast to her pliant sister, Julia, who slides from one self-centered mistress-role to another whenever "profligate debasement assumed the mask of pleasure" (145). Although both these lives are clearly performative ones, despite her occasionally claiming the "gift of Nature" (which the narrator finds in her acting [84]), Martha's roles are the ones that keep opening female opportunities beyond repeated captivity by men. Through this character, Robinson's "identity" as "the sum total of the scripts she performed" (Mellor 256) is genuinely celebrated for much of this novel, making identity-by-performance, though beset by struggle and prejudice, an emerging female heroism not attempted by Ann Radcliffe, with the Gothic surfacing only rarely to unsettle this performance of gender.

Nevertheless, the Gothic does haunt *The Natural Daughter*. The occasional passages where it appears do temper this novel's intermittent, if anguished, hopefulness with the Walpolean power of ancient schemes recast in counterfeited forms to still bedevil modern attempts to break out of older molds. In one such episode, Martha is kidnapped by masked men in the dark and taken to "a large old-fashioned" building that turns out to be a "private mad-house" where she is soon "bled, blistered, menaced, and tortured" (WMR 7: 140–141). As Hester Davenport has seen (7: 356 n.5), even though such institutions did horrifically exist, Robinson is here alluding most immediately to Wollstonecraft's fervently Gothic, albeit unfinished, novel *The Wrongs of Woman,* which Godwin published with other *Memoirs* of his late wife in 1798. In this "Fragment" (Wollstonecraft 1980: 69), the heroine, "Maria," all too sane, is condemned to a "huge pile of buildings" with "turrets" where "warring elements" in its mixture of rebuilding and "decay" have become analogous to the "groans and shrieks" of the inmates who now fill its vacated space and so create a modern "prison" where the subterranean dungeons of the ancient past have expanded from below to subsume a whole structure for the modern purposes of culling the "insane" from the "sane" (1980: 75–77). Here we find that the heroine has been consigned to this repurposed Gothic pile by "the selfish schemes" of "her husband" to pull her regressively toward traditional subordination and to extrapolate such backslidings to keep "the world a vast prison" into which all "women" are "born slaves" (1980: 76, 79). Martha's incarceration in *The Natural Daughter*, though, while certainly extending these associations, does not attribute a cause to any individual. Instead, when she requests a "book for her amusement," she is given one of "her own" novels as if being a "crazy woman who fancies herself an authoress" is "to be in the most decided state of raving insanity" (*WMR* 7: 141). The independent woman writer, this Gothic episode suggests, is often publicly counterfeited, even monsterized, as a criminal or a madwoman and then thrown away, by gossip or criticism or the literary marketplace, into a pre-Enlightenment darkness where the remade husks of a male-dominated past keep striving to resubsume and silence her. Following up on Wollstonecraft turning the terrors-in-castle-depths of Walpole's and Radcliffe's women into the broadly institutionalized, if antiquated, subjugation of women across the Western world, Robinson's *Natural Daughter* foregrounds the threat that haunts emergent female creativity with the ever-looming chance that all the expansions in modern female roles in this novel, difficult as they already are, can be reversed by ubiquitous male power using towering old structures as repositories for their newest dominations.

An equally unsettling Gothic episode in this novel is another, yet quite different, echo of an episode in *The Wrongs of Woman.* Just as Maria's attendant at the asylum in Wollstonecraft's fragment, Jemima, tells her dark story of becoming "utterly destitute" (Wollstonecraft 1980: 102–120), the real mother of Fanny, who calls herself "Mrs. Sedgley" (a stage name) and is Martha's mentor in acting (*WMR* 7: 68), recounts her own past journey to the abject poverty in which she gave up her child to Martha (7: 69–79). In *The Wrongs'* inserted narrative, though it anticipates Mrs. Sedgley's when Jemima finds herself "with child" by an upper-class man and is able to develop an "active mind" despite her "inequality of condition" (Wollstonecraft 1980: 107, 111, 113), the emphasis is on the oppressive setting of the working classes that forces them into gendered performances, sinking countless women to "the servility of a slave," with Jemima so Gothically "forrow[ed]" by these horrors that her face acquires "a sort of supernatural wildness" (1980: 103). Mrs. Sedgley's tale begins at a more upper-class level, because of which her account becomes more Gothic from the start, and it stays with that mode even when it becomes openly current to the 1790s. Born to a father "proud even to imperious tyranny" in his alpha-male performance, Mrs. Sedgley as a child is told she will be taken to his "Gothic castle" in Scotland, where she fears she will be subjected to such male domin- ation, reinforced by "legends so terrific," that her mind will be attacked by "all the horrors of romance" (WMR 7: 69–70), the "dark Gothic" side of a Castle of Otranto. She gains some respite from having to perform this now-standard female role when she becomes a "companion" to "a woman of rank" eager to visit the continent, but she soon learns that this lady ultimately plans to return her to her father, whereupon "all the visionary horrors of Drumbender Castle" loom up again in her mind, and she foresees the future performance of her womanhood as that of a "pale ghost" buried in "subterraneous caverns" like Walpole's Isabella (7: 70).

But on the journey back to Britain through Paris, during which she meets the "traveler" who will father Fanny, she is stopped and captured by the Revolution, now violently active. It is a chaotic "plenitude of dominion," where an anarchic "excess of horror" makes her "sigh for the solitudes of Drumbender," compared to which, since she has only imagined that "Gothic castle," the Revolution's imprisonment of her, now in a real "subterraneous dungeon," seems far more threatening (7: 71–72) now that she is physically playing a part very like Isabella's in *Otranto* and Emily's in *Udolpho*. Worse yet, the tyranny she mostly imagines in her patriarch's retreat is transferred over to a "monster" who now lords threats of the guillotine over her and many others while disguised as a "son of Liberty" (talk about the specter of a counterfeit!); he turns out to be "the despot Marat" himself, who offers to free Martha with a "demonian" gaze, echoing *The Monk's* Lucifer (Lewis 243–244), if she will be his sex slave like *The Monk's* Matilda (*WMR* 7: 73) so he can enact one of the most controlling male performances there is. Fortunately for Martha, the historical reality of Marat's "death on the following day" at the hands of Charlotte Corday (July 13, 1793, when the real man was too ill to attempt interrogation and seduction [7: 347 n.103]), leads to Mrs. Sedgley's release and, unfortunately, her return to

England as a cast-off, then an increasingly impoverished, fallen woman (7: 73–79). This is the role in which Martha finds her, a condition like Jemima's throughout most of *her* tale, and that similarity makes the performances of female degradation by all three women much more similar – and more like Corday's journey from counter-revolution to the guillotine – than their different backgrounds might have normally made them. As Setzer rightly observes about *The Natural Daughter*, Robinson here uses blatantly fictional Gothic, deliberately changing history, to make "Jacobin terrorism" the "dark double" of English patriarchal power as it is imaginatively reinforced by the ancient "horrors of romance" (Robinson 2003: 31). Women's attempts to change their roles, whether they are Martha's or Mrs. Sedgley's or Jemima's or Maria's, are still for Robinson, even in 1799, enveloped by pervasive old practices of determined male dominance, familial and political. The Gothic, though this novel resists it at times, invades *The Natural Daughter* enough to show that its struggles toward the expansion of womanhood exist in an environment of hauntingly retrograde forces in a tug-of-war that only the Gothic can capture with the full Walpolean force of its Janus-faced aesthetic.

7 The Gothic in *Lyrical Tales*

This dynamic, as I have begun to suggest earlier, finally joins Robinson's poetry thoroughly in many of the pieces she chose for her *Lyrical Tales*, published just a month before her death, and here the ideological conflicts that the Gothic helps expose are sometimes similar to and sometimes different from the ones she intimates in her novels. Most of the poems in the *Tales* first appeared separately in London's *Morning Post* as parts of a printed conversation among poets, in which Robinson placed herself in dialogue with William Wordsworth and especially Samuel Taylor Coleridge, among others (see Cross 2017: 28–50). Moreover, as scholars have already shown (especially Curran 22–25 and Cross 166–189), the *Lyrical Tales* are a direct answer, often poem-for-poem, to Wordsworth and Coleridge's *Lyrical Ballads* of 1798, for many still the most "founding" volume in the development of English Romanticism. The challenges Robinson poses to that iconic collection, in part with her only half-similar title, take many forms as she pointedly counters the pursuit of a transcendental Romanticism in the *Ballads* poems. First, she draws the *Ballads* claim of a "new realism" in poetry toward the more vernacular "materialism" of Robert Southey's *English Eclogues* (1799) to highlight the "endemic injustice and abuse of power . . . thwarting [the] potentiality" of the war-torn and the dispossessed of the 1790s, figures whom several *Ballads* strive to ennoble by emphasizing the power of the mind over meager material conditions (Curran 23–26). Second, the

Tales undercut the *Ballads'* attempt at "conceptual homogeneity" by employing a wider profusion of "stanzaic and sonic patterns" (Curran 27). These expand the number of perspectives through which readers can see, among other inequities, "the trauma and isolation that young people and women experience" (Cross 179). Third, Robinson signals with *Tales* in her title that the frequent drive in the *Ballads* to make the lyric rise out of sensation and temporal life toward a "spirit healed and harmonized/By the benignant touch of love and beauty" – words from Coleridge's "The Dungeon" in the 1798 *Ballads* (ll. 29–30; Coleridge and Wordsworth 114) – can and should be brought more to earth by the temporality of "narrative" stories-in-verse that detail "personal histor[ies]" of the "gross realities" of 1790s Britain that were and remain wrenchingly "at odds with Wordsworth's idealization of the figures of humble, rural life" (Bolton 743–748).

Yet all of these disarticulations in the *Tales*, I would argue, are often bound up with and filtered through the Gothic, which is what most allows Robinson to suggest deeper levels of Janus-faced inconsistency in what this collection half-echoes from the *Ballads*. To be sure, the Walpolean Gothic by this time had become both commonplace and condemned in many literary circles. Coleridge excoriates it as a "low and vulgar" mix of incompatible styles in his 1797 review of *The Monk* (Clery and Miles 2000: 187), and Wordsworth will go on, in his Preface to the Second Edition of *Lyrical Ballads* (1801), to include the Gothic among the "deluges of idle and extravagant stories" that the *Ballads* were fashioned to rise above in their manifestations of a more "discriminating" and "organic sensibility." Even so, Robinson surely recognized that Coleridge and Wordsworth used the Walpolean Gothic themselves in their 1798 collection, the former in "The Rime of the Ancyent Marinere" and the latter in "The Thorn" at least (Coleridge and Wordsworth 2008: 49–72, 103–110; see Miles 2008: 80–83, 131–132). Her *Tales* consequently force them to confront the unresolved inconsistencies in their own poetic agendas, thereby exposing the ancient-versus-modern undercurrents within one *Ballads* poem after another. Robinson's *Tales* do not merely play out her preference for what the *Ballads* authors claim to reject. By calling forth the more sublimated Gothic already lurking in the *Ballads*, she makes it act as a haunting specter that undermines – or, more precisely, unearths the half-buried ideological conflicts in – the attempts at uplifting imaginative coalescence in that famous collection.

"All Alone"

Robinson's opening lyric in the *Tales*, for example, "All Alone" (*WMR* 2: 146–150), responds to Wordsworth's "We Are Seven" in the 1798 *Ballads* (Coleridge and Wordsworth 100–102). In the latter, the eight-year-old girl beheld by the speaker somewhere near a "Church-yard" demonstrates her native powers of imagination, which the poem finally celebrates in the face of her many losses, by speaking of all six of her siblings as present, still together at a level that transcends one place, even though all of them are absent, two of them within visible graves that are now "green" and "Beneath the church-yard tree" (ll. 21, 32, 37). By contrast, the speaker who addresses the orphan boy in "All Alone" laments that "Thy cheek is now grown deathly pale," as though the lad were a ghostly Gothic figure hovering between the living and the dead (l. 20). Robinson's speaker even adds that "Thy pillow now [is] a cold grave stone" (ll. 28–29), as if the boy can sleep only on the slab where his mother's corpse lies buried; he is almost indistinguishable from that body which "withers under yon grave stone," even as he withers too while the dead mother "sleeps" just on the other side of the same "pillow" (ll. 11, 29). Besides suggesting the starvation of abandoned country children that Wordsworth fails to mention in "We Are Seven," this image-cluster sees the foundation of the orphan's loneliness as blurring the conventional boundaries between life and death. Robinson's child thus described carries suggestions beyond those in the graveyard poetry that she once favored. He is and is not already a ghost, already half-dead, and the distance between his bed and his mother's is only the short one between two sides of one-and-the-same gravestone. It is as if he is a young *Otranto* specter from whom the past is increasingly absent yet who counterfeits death in his betwixt-and-between present while moving forward toward death and the past at the same time.

Among the implications here, as we look back at *Lyrical Ballads* through the filter of *Lyrical Tales*, is that the child of "We Are Seven" could not place her absent siblings on the same level with herself if she were not fully analogous to them. She inclines, like Robinson's orphan, toward their death-state *and* toward the lost past when they were all in one location, while she also maintains their one-time, current, and future presence as equivalent to hers. The Gothic over-tones muted, though still present, in the "church-yard" and "graves" in "We Are Seven," and possibly the six ghosts that the girl sees standing beside her, are brought into the foreground of Robinson's "All Alone." As a result, their ghostliness and their pull toward the past are transferred into the "All Alone" orphan himself, into his looking ahead in a repetitive way that can connect the future only to the losses in his past that have left him alone until he dies. This conundrum then sets the stage – since Robinson, the one-time actress, cannot resist making this boy the speaker of a soliloquy in a scene set decisively "by the Church-yard side" (l. 1) – for multiple narrative flashbacks about those he has lost (ll. 73–114) that convey far more temporality and retrospection than we find in "We Are Seven." Reinforced by these ghost-like story-portraits, the boy in *Lyrical Tales* continually finishing his stanzas with "ALONE" becomes even more of a Janus-faced specter, looking backward at the deaths of his mother and others and forward at the lonely span between his current aporia and his being finally pulled into death and the past with them. He thereby helps us now see Wordsworth's "cottage girl" as really this kind of figure too (Coleridge and Wordsworth 2008: 100, l. 5). In making Robinson's orphan boy a living-dead shade, as well as Janus-faced, on a Gothicized stage set, the *Lyrical Tales* are looking back *and* making the *Lyrical Ballads* look back to the tug-of-war in the Gothic mixture of genres inaugurated by Walpole's *Otranto* over four decades earlier.

By placing this boy in a theatricalized space, moreover, Robinson also raises the question for her and us – and hence for *Lyrical Ballads* – that arises from the theatricality of the Gothic in Walpole and his progeny: are motivations formed internally, by way of Lockean perception and associations over time, or are they formed performatively, by actions, reactions, and counterreactions, mostly in the theatrical give-and-take of a visible external world – or are both operating at once? With the girl in "We Are Seven," the *Ballads* try to make the imaginative presence of her siblings grow only out of her internal gatherings of memories. In "All Alone," it is hard to decide whether the orphan's "looks forlorn" (l. 21), behind which we never see because we only hear what he says (as in a theater), result from all that has been done to him from outside him (as "Fate had left thee," l. 18) or from his internal reactions to the series of deprivations that make up his experience (which perhaps he *chooses* to think of as leading to one end: "When I am hid in yonder grave!" [l. 148]). For readers of *Lyrical Ballads* through the overlay of *Lyrical Tales*, that hesitation between different roots of thought now inhabits the depiction of the girl in "We Are Seven," who is as theatrical as she is imaginative, placed as she is in a dramatic dialogue with the speaker and described by him as Godwinian, infused by her "rustic, woodland" setting as any mind is by its surroundings (Coleridge and Wordsworth 100, l. 9). Robinson thereby points to a Gothic subtext within Wordsworthian Romantic quests, in which identity is torn between conflicting ideologies about them around 1800, much as the Gothic was when Walpole established his "new species of romance" in 1764–5.

Robinson, I would also argue, takes this suggestion of unresolved conflict even further. When she has her "All Alone" speaker, on the one hand, highlight the boy's luxuriant "hair/In silky waves" (ll. 13–14) and call him to "rustic sport" on "yonder hill" (ll. 43–44), the poem invokes the age-old imagery of pastoral romance, including how such a romance hero usually looks, hearkening all the way back to the orphan-shepherd who is really noble in the ancient Greek *Daphnis and Chloe* of Longus (second century AD; see Longus 4–7) and reappearing in the country peasant who turns out to be the heir to the castle in Walpole's *Otranto*. On the other hand, the same speaker turns just as much to a graphic realism that refers us to our immediate senses and to hard facts about English poverty in the 1790s, as in "Thy naked feet are wounded sore/With naked thorns" (ll. 25–26). The speaker momentarily, yes, invokes a barefoot Christ on the road to Calvary crowned with thorns, but only as (literally) stripped down without any suggestion of a future Resurrection or any discovery of a Daphnis' noble birth. In this and other such juxtapositions, Robinson is echoing Walpole's definition of the Gothic as oscillating between the ancient and the modern. There could hardly be a more self-divided aesthetic mode and hence none more suited to manifesting Janus-faced tugs of war between retrograde and progressive systems of belief in the Western culture of the 1790s. These are what she sees as underlying Wordsworth's perceptions of abject poverty when she draws on the Gothic in the first poem of *Lyrical Tales* to suggest that the same indecision really underpins "All Alone," her *Tales*, "We Are Seven," and the *Lyrical Ballads* alike. The orphan in "All Alone" may be called toward the world of pastoral romance but sees that option as his author does, quite Gothically: as distant, dated, and empty for him in a world of lingering class structures that have helped to cast him from a family-life of at least subsistence to a solitude of destitution, especially by "modern" standards.

"The Poor, Singing Dame"

The Gothic call to past structures and symbols for Robinson is, after all, a pull toward retrograde social orders that are indeed philosophically groundless because they are fundamentally oppressive, inequitable, and exploitative of poor children, unpropertied men, and of course women, such as she has become as a "fallen" female degraded from being a Prince's consort to "singing for her supper" in print. In "The Poor, Singing Dame" also in her *Tales* (*WMR* 2: 33–34), an answer to Wordsworth's "The Female Vagrant" in the 1798 *Ballads* (Coleridge and Wordsworth 81–89) – where the title figure, also the main speaker, blames herself "that I have my inner self abused" (89, l. 259) – Robinson opens with a stark juxtaposition already familiar to her long-time readers: an "old Castle ... haunted, and dreary" set right next to a "poor little hovel" (ll. 1, 13). In the latter, a cheerful "old Dame ... would merrily sing" as she works making food and clothing, with such resonance that she fills the Castle's empty "rich chambers" with sounds that increase their "haunted," and thus sepulchral, quality (ll. 19–20, 13). "The Lord of the Castle," envious of her happiness and tormented by her voice in the face of his empty, half-dead existence, dispatches an "old Steward" to take her to a quick death in "Prison" (ll. 34–40) in an exercise of blatant aristocratic, as well as patriarchal, authority, for which *this* female bears no blame at all. Such a move is reminiscent, certainly, of the Prince of Wales in his dealings with Robinson (the "old Dame" *is* named "MARY," l. 50), but also of Prince Manfred's medieval killing of the one woman who has most defied his authority (who tragically turns out to be his daughter) in Walpole's *Otranto*. The consequences of this brutality, while recognizably recent, therefore remain partly within the world of "ancient romance," as do the performances of gender it plays out. From the "fatal moment" of old Mary's passing, the Lord is haunted by "Screech-owls appalling," reminiscent of the avenging female Furies in Aeschylus' ancient Greek *Orestia*, and, because they "shriek like a ghost," the Lord recalls the "All Alone" orphan in becoming ghost-like himself, "His bones … wasting, his flesh … decaying" (ll. 56–61) as he descends into a grave finally placed beside old Mary's: a masculine "tomb of rich marble" that now "O'ershadows" her simple feminine plot much as the castle towered over the hovel, save that both characters are now equal in being dead and buried (ll. 63–64). Such imagery intensifies the speaker's memory in Wordsworth's "Vagrant" that a "mansion proud" rose up in the "woods" surrounding her and her shepherd-father's "nook," whereupon the new "master" tried to buy their land and, when the father refused, his "troubles grew" until "all his substance fell into decay" and "All was seized," leaving the daughter homeless (Coleridge and Wordsworth 83, ll. 39–53). Robinson's riposte has this kind of power-play descend on the woman directly. She thereby draws the "Vagrant" story Gothically back toward the age-old class inequities behind it, turning this conflict into a spectral presence from the dark ages that is actually haunting Wordsworth's poem just as much as it bedevils "The Poor Singing Dame."

Whatever the post-medieval poetic justice for an eighteenth-century woman that may be achieved by this "haunting," though, the Gothic in this Robinson poem, as in others, clearly does not want to leave the ancient Janus-face behind. The remembered stability of supernatural retribution, with owls assumed for centuries to be omens of impending death for the sinful, has again provided an *old*-world Gothic solution for inequalities of rank and gender that have lasted until the 1790s, even while they are now being questioned by Robinson, Godwin, Wollstonecraft, and others as devoid of lasting substance. Such moments establish what the conflicted quintessence of Gothic melancholy comes to be for Robinson by the late 1790s, as we have seen in *The False Friend* and her *Memoirs*. Like the terror-based "sublime" of Burke, the Gothic for her is a compelling articulation of humanity's passage from and through, while also being held within, the ruins of a crumbling but still-compelling past. The remains of these monuments do pull us toward their fearful deathliness and false promises of age-old certainty. But they can also be seen to be giving way, if only just, to more enlightened and as-yet unfinished reconstructions that resist them – the Protestant order incorporating and then surpassing the Catholic one, as in the Bristol Minster, or the scandalous royal mistress who became a major traditional *and* nontraditional writer – all by way of aesthetic constructs underwritten by the Gothic as a *différend*, among them, she presumes, her "melancholy" works and the *Lyrical Ballads* as well.

"The Alien Boy"

No poem exemplifies this sense of the Gothic's recollective and revisionary power more than the variation on "All Alone" placed near the conclusion of Robinson's *Tales*: "The Alien Boy" (*WMR* 2: 172–175), a reaction mainly to Wordsworth's "The Idiot Boy" in the 1798 *Ballads* (Coleridge and Wordsworth 119–132). In Wordsworth's piece, country mother Betty Foy, on a "March night" when an "owlet . . . Shouts from nobody knows where," sends her "half-wise" son, Johnny, on horseback "To bring a doctor from the town,/To comfort poor old Susan Gale," the sick neighbor to whom Betty is tending, and Johnny never reaches the doctor because he gives way to his horse's instinct to stop and graze by a "roaring water-fall" (ll. 1–4, 198, 130–131, 357–370). Because of his delay, parodies of anxious Gothic imagery, based mostly on country superstitions, rise up in the thoughts of Betty, Susan, and even the speaker/narrator, who speculates that Johnny might have become "like a silent horseman-ghost" (l. 335). But Johnny himself, finally discovered "upright on a feeding horse" like a miraculous apparition "such [as] we in romances read" (ll. 361–365), is so entirely free of such hauntings in his innocent imaginings within nature that all he can say, having "heard/The owls in tuneful concert," is "The cocks did crow to-whoo, to whoo" (ll. 452–459). He returns us to the poem's beginning as though he were transforming it from ominous to playful, but in a projection-ahead where night becomes day and the sun is just rising. The hauntings of old Gothic fears can be left behind, it would seem, in native, natural poetry uttered by a youth whose "idiocy" is really akin to a world-renewing Romantic imagination.

Robinson's "Alien Boy," in contrast, attaches Gothicism and its associations with violent and "sublime" historical change firmly to her title figure and thereby recovers Gothicism from Wordsworth's semi-satire on it, ultimately drawing attention to the Gothic undercurrents in "The Idiot Boy" itself. Her lad, "HENRY," who has lived for years on a "Mountain" near England's "Western" coast with his father, "saint HUBERT," a fugitive from the French Revolution (an unabashed extension of Robinson's Hubert de Sevrac), has long wanted to know from Hubert the history that brought them to where they are, even if it means learning of "Proud mansions, rich domains, and joyous scenes/Forever

faded" (ll. 1, 10, 42–43). His father, after all, is the saintly image of the other that
defines his son in having crossed from older world into a brave new one. But the
completion of this boy's Janus-faced transition from a dying past to a bright
future is arrested by Saint Hubert's drowning in a "wide domain of howling
Death" as he strives to rescue a "poor shipwreck'd Man" from a storm at sea (ll.
62, 77). Right at that moment, Henry is "fear struck, e'en to madness," hearing
little more than "the wisp'ring of a million souls/Beneath the green-deep
mourning" of the churning ocean (ll. 93–104), an echo of Coleridge's
"Ancyent Marinere," which begins the 1798 *Ballads* (Coleridge and
Wordsworth 2008: 62–63, ll. 319–342). This boy's mental longing for history,
with his defining other and teacher about the past so suddenly wrenched from
him, dissolves into a haunting, vague intimation (the "million souls") of all the
lives lost in the French Revolution, its aftermath, or perhaps all of history, and
even this *mélange*, while echoing in the waves, is sinking from his awareness as
he contemplates it. The Lockean "tablet of his mind" is consequently "disorder'd, chang'd,/Fading" (ll. 124–125), a Gothic state of thought like many in
Robinson's novels but even more extreme, in which the psyche is suspended
between fragmentary remnants of the receded past and an unknown future
where "disorder'd" memories remain as a "whispering" intermixture of different older voices that cannot be disentangled.

The alien boy thus remains, like the lad in "All Alone," a half-dead
Walpolean specter that both longs for and has lost contact with his past
groundings, "A maniac wild" who is "melancholy proof that Man may bear/
All the rude storms of Fate, and still suspire,/By the world forgotten" (ll. 122,
133–134). In one belief-system, he is the victim of a primordial Fate beyond
human understanding while, in another, he is the product of human decisions to
neglect and forget masses of dispossessed people. Extending tendencies in
many other figures of hers, Robinson's alien boy haunts us since 1800, like
her *Tales*, with the foregrounded symbol of a *différend* culture suspended
between the haunting past, the too-real present, unknown possibilities, and
ideological conflicts about how to view all of it. While those levels seem
transcended by the reassuring tone in Wordsworth's "Idiot Boy," they are
actually there in the figure of "old Susan" for whom Johnny is sent to find
a doctor; while "her body" does get "better" without assistance, her "mind grew
worse and worse" because of myriad "doubts and terrors" in both her imagination and her feelings about her diseased and deprived social condition
(Coleridge and Wordsworth 2008: 131, ll. 422–426). The attempted rising
beyond the Gothic in "The Idiot Boy," if we look at it through Robinson's
poetic alternative, has been brought back to the unresolved conflicts Gothically
simmering deep in its world. This revelation in the *Lyrical Tales*, in its very

Gothicism and like so many of Robinson's published works, powerfully fashions a figure for the fugitive and dispossessed who, in her eyes, have accumulated all across European history, culminating in the extensive deprivation of the 1790s, at least in part because of the irresolutions between ancient and modern thinking that, for her, have had to be symbolized in Western culture by the Walpolean Gothic mode to which she has devoted so much of her prolific writing.

8 Coda

Such exposures of underlying cultural aporias appear prominently – and Gothically – in many other *Lyrical Tales*, especially "The Haunted Beach" (Robinson's principal counter to the "Ancyent Marinere"; *WMR* 2: 44–46; see Aguirre), "The Deserted Cottage" (2: 60–61), "Poor Marguerite" (2: 76–77), "The Lascar," "The Widow's Home," "The Fugitive," "The Negro Girl," "The Trumpeter, an Old English Tale," and "Golfre, a Gothic Swiss Tale" (these last six printed successively in 2: 150–189). I invite my readers to explore the Gothic implications in all of these, I hope through the lenses I have argued for here. These pieces, written over the same years as their author's *Memoirs*, continue what we find in almost every use of the Gothic by Mary Darby Robinson: the tension between the lingering force of age-old beliefs or icons and progressive critiques of these that strive to open up alternative ways of being for everyone, especially women and other dispossessed people. Robinson had no doubt that she was employing the Gothic to question and undermine traditional assumptions and the horrors they too often generate, building on what Walpole, Radcliffe, and others, as she saw them, began to do before her. In *Walsingham*, she has her title character's landlady attempt, much like Robinson, to be an author crossing many literary genres even though "Mrs. Wofford" constantly faces, like her writer as the 1790s wore on, the determination among "all the docile danglers of the *haut ton* to ridicule the petticoat pedant" and enlist the "popular newspapers" to do so as well (*WMR* 5: 192). These efforts by Mrs. Wofford include "a Romance of most terrific intensity!," a "book of terrors" that critics find to be a "heterogenous mass" (5: 193), perhaps not surprisingly given the Gothic's conflation of inherently incompatible genres. Even so, again like her author, this doughty landlady persists, even to the point of combining this mode with "modern Comedy," as we have seen Robinson do. The result – of which both Robinson and her avatar are manifestly proud – is a public product "*Gothic enough* to utter truths which offended the pride of elegant insignificance," so much so that an influential "hag of distinction" sees "every line" to be a too-revealing "mirror which reflected her own deformity"

(5: 194, my emphasis). This reaction is the sign of a conflicted social order that too often uses antiquated, now-hollow "distinction" to stifle critiques that suggest the possibilities of a more equitable world and an uplifted state of mind, such as the "mournful meditation" that Robinson regarded as her highest condition, in part because of her birth in a Gothic setting. This paradox is what the Gothic, itself a paradoxical mode, could best address in her eyes, and, right up until she died with her Gothic *Memoirs* unfinished, she wrote in this way again and again, certainly to earn money and to justify her own existence, but also to help transform her culture to face its contradictions and, as a result, to better embrace and do greater justice to all those it now dispossesses.

Bibliography

Aguirre, Manuel, "Mary Robinson's 'The Haunted Beach' and the Grammar of Gothic," *Neophilologus* 98 (2014): 689–704.

Baudrillard, Jean, *Symbolic Exchange and Death*, trans. Iain Hamilton Grant (London: Sage, 1993).

Bolton, Betsy, "Romancing the Stone: 'Perdita' Robinson in Wordsworth's London," *English Literary History* 64: 3 (1997): 727–759.

Brewer, William D., "Copies, Protean Role-Players, and Sappho's Shattered Form in Mary Robinson's *The False Friend*," *European Romantic Review* 22: 6 (2011): 785–800.

Brewer, William D., "The French Revolution as a Romance: Mary Robinson's *Hubert de Sevrac*," *Papers on Language and Literature* 42: 2 (2006): 115–149.

Castle, Terry, "The Spectralization of the Other in *The Mysteries of Udolpho*," in Felicity Nussbaum and Laura Brown (eds.), *The New Eighteenth Century: Theory, Politics, English Literature* (New York: Methuen, 1987), pp. 231–253.

Chandler, James, *An Archeology of Sympathy: The Sentimental Mode in Literature and Cinema* (Chicago: University of Chicago Press, 2013).

Clery, Emma J., "Horace Walpole's *The Mysterious Mother* and the Impossibility of Female Desire," in Fred Botting (ed.), *Essays and Studies 2001: The Gothic* (Cambridge: D.S. Brewer, 2002), pp. 23–46.

Clery, E. J., *The Rise of Supernatural Fiction, 1762–1800* (Cambridge: Cambridge University Press, 1995).

Clery, E. J., and Robert Miles (eds.), *Gothic Documents: A Sourcebook, 1700–1820* (Manchester: Manchester University Press, 2000).

Close, Anne, "Notorious: Mary Robinson and the Gothic," *Gothic Studies* 6: 2 (2004): 172–191.

Coleridge, Samuel Taylor, and William Wordsworth, *Lyrical Ballads 1798 and 1800*, edited by Michael Gamer and Dahlia Porter (Peterborough, Ont: Broadview, 2008).

Cross, Ashley, *Mary Robinson and the Genesis of Romanticism: Literary Dialogues and Debts, 1784–1821* (London: Routledge, 2017).

Curran, Stuart, "Mary Robinson's *Lyrical Tales* in Context," in Carol Shiner and Joel Hoefner (eds.), *Revisioning Romanticism: British Women Writers, 1776–1837* (Philadelphia: University of Pennsylvania Press, 1994), pp. 17–35.

Freud, Sigmund, "Mourning and Melancholia," in *The Standard Edition of the Complete Psychological Works*, ed. and trans. James Strachey et al. (London: Hogarth Press, 1953–1974), vol. 14, pp.243–258.

Frye, Roland Mushat, *The Renaissance Hamlet: Issues and Responses in 1600* (Princeton: Princeton University Press, 1984).

Godwin, William, *Caleb Williams*, edited by Pamela Clemit (Oxford: Oxford University Press, 2009).

Godwin, William, *Enquiry Concerning Political Justice*, edited by Isaac Kramnick (Harmondsworth: Penguin, 1976).

Groom, Nick, *The Gothic: A Very Short Introduction* (Oxford: Oxford University Press, 2012).

Hogle, Jerrold E., "The Ghost of the Counterfeit in the Genesis of the Gothic," in Allan Lloyd Smith and Victor Sage (eds.), *Gothick Origins and Innovations* (Amsterdam: Rodopi, 1994), pp. 23–33.

Hogle, Jerrold E., "The Gothic-Romantic Hybridity in Mary Robinson's *Lyrical Tales*," *The European Legacy* 24: 3–4 (2019): 24–34.

Lewis, Matthew Gregory, *The Monk*, edited by David L. Macdonald and Kathleen Scherf (Peterborough, Ont.: Broadview, 2004).

Locke, John, *An Essay Concerning Human Understanding*, edited by Peter H. Nidditch (Oxford: Clarendon Press, 1979).

Longus, *The Pastorals, or the Loves of Daphnis and Chloe: The Athenian Society Translation* (Cambridge, Ontario: In parentheses, 2002).

Lyotard, Jean François, *The Differend: Phrases in Dispute*, translated by George Van Den Abbeele (Minneapolis: University of Minnesota Press, 1988).

McGann, Jerome, *The Poetics of Sensibility: A Revolution in Literary Style* (Oxford: Clarendon, 1996).

Mellor, Anne K., "Mary Robinson and the Scripts of Female Sexuality," in Patrick Coleman, Jayne Elizabeth Lewis, and Jill Anne Kowalik (eds.), *Representations of the Self from the Renaissance to Romanticism* (Cambridge: Cambridge University Press, 2000), pp. 230–259.

Miles, Robert, *Romantic Misfits* (London: Palgrave Macmillan, 2008).

Morris, David B., "Gothic Sublimity," *New Literary History* 16: 2 (1985): 299–219.

Poovey, Mary, "Ideology and 'The Mysteries of Udolpho'," *Criticism* 2: 4 (1979): 307–330.

Radcliffe, Ann, *A Sicilian Romance*, edited by Alison Milbank (Oxford: Oxford University Press, 1993).

Radcliffe, Ann, *The Italian*, edited by Frederick Garber and Emma J. Clery (Oxford: Oxford University Press, 1998*a*).

Radcliffe, Ann, *The Mysteries of Udolpho*, edited by Bonamy Dobrée and Terry Castle (Oxford: Oxford University Press, 1998*b*).

Robinson, Mary, *A Letter to the Women of England and The Natural Daughter*, edited by Sharon M. Setzer (Peterborough, Ont.: Broadview, 2003).

Robinson, Mary, *Selected Poems*, edited by Judith Pascoe (Peterborough, Ont.: Broadview, 2000).

Russo, Stephanie, "History Repeating: Mothers, Daughters, and Incest in Mary Robinson's *Vancenza* and *The False Friend*," *Tulsa Studies in Women's Literature* 37: 1 (2018): 67–90.

Shaffer, Julie, "*Walsingham*: Gender, Pain, Knowledge," *Women's Writing* 9: 1 (2002): 69–85.

Sedgwick, Eve Kosofsky, "The Character in the Veil: Imagery of the Surface in the Gothic Novel," *Publications of the Modern Language Association of America* 96: 2 (1981): 255–270.

Setzer, Sharon M., "The Gothic Structure of Mary Robinson's *Memoirs*," in Eugene Stelzig (ed.), *Romantic Autobiography in England* (Farnham: Ashgate, 2009), pp. 31–47.

Shakespeare, William, *The Riverside Shakespeare*, edited by G. Blakemore Evans et al. (Boston: Houghton Mifflin, 1974).

Spenser, Edmund, *Edmund Spenser's Poetry*, edited by Hugh Maclean (New York: Norton, 1968).

Storch, Rudolf F., "Metaphors of Private Guilt and Social Rebellion in Godwin's *Caleb Williams*," *English Literary History* 34: 2 (1967): 188–207.

Taylor, Charles, *A Secular Age* (Cambridge, MA: Harvard University Press, 2007).

Townshend, Dale, *Gothic Antiquity: History, Romance, and the Architectural Imagination, 1760–1840* (Oxford: Oxford University Press, 2019).

Ty, Eleanor, *Empowering the Feminine: The Narratives of Mary Robinson, Jane West, and Amelia Opie, 1796–1812* (Toronto: University of Toronto Press, 1998).

Walpole, Horace, *The Castle of Otranto and The Mysterious Mother*, edited by Frederick S. Frank (Peterborough, Ont.: Broadview, 2003).

Walpole, Horace, *The Letters of Horace Walpole*, 4 vols. (Dinslaken: Anboco, 2016). E-Book.

Wollstonecraft, Mary, *A Vindication of the Rights of Woman*, edited by Charles Hagelman (New York: Norton, 1967).

Wollstonecraft, Mary, *Maria and The Wrongs of Woman*, edited by Gary Kelly (Oxford: Oxford University Press, 1980).

Acknowledgments

I am deeply grateful to the highly supportive general editors of the *Elements in the Gothic* series, the excellent Cambridge UP staff, my colleagues in the International Gothic Association and the Gothic Scholars group, and my wonderful family. Portions of this Element are derived from an article of mine published in *The European Legacy* journal on January 21, 2019 (DOI: http://10.1080/10848770.2018.1562665), and I am much obliged to Taylor and Francis Online for granting me permission to include this material.

Cambridge Elements ☰

The Gothic

Dale Townshend
Manchester Metropolitan University
Dale Townshend is Professor of Gothic Literature in the Manchester Centre for Gothic Studies, Manchester Metropolitan University.

Angela Wright
University of Sheffield
Angela Wright is Professor of Romantic Literature in the School of English at the University of Sheffield and codirector of its Centre for the History of the Gothic.

Advisory Board

About the Series

Seeking to publish short, research-led yet accessible studies of the foundational 'elements' within Gothic Studies as well as showcasing new and emergent lines of scholarly enquiry, this innovative series brings to a range of specialist and non-specialist readers some of the most exciting developments in recent Gothic scholarship.

Cambridge Elements ☰

The Gothic

Elements in the Series